Praise for
The Cost of Capitalism

"As an investment professional who's worked in both public policy and financial markets, Bob's book elegantly dissects and explains the dynamics of the Wall Street–Washington axis."
—**Jeffrey Applegate,** Chief Investment Officer,
Global Wealth Management

"*The Cost of Capitalism* is a must-read—and a thoroughly enjoyable one—for those who want to understand the Crisis of 2008 and hammer out a new framework for decision making."
—**Jared L. Cohon,** President, Carnegie Mellon University

"In a world of false philosophers, Bob Barbera has distinguished himself by delivering real value. With this book, he puts blood back into the veins of high finance by building a model centered on the human capacity for error. Readers who absorb its lessons will be armed with more than mere technique; they will acquire an attitude that will make them better investors for the rest of their lives."
—**Paul DeRosa,** Principal, Mt. Lucas Management Corp.

"Bob Barbera has refined a keen Minskyite perspective over many successful years on Wall Street. This book is filled with valuable insights on the financial boom and bust cycles that have left many of us scratching our heads."
—**Jon Faust,** Director, Center for Financial Economics,
Department of Economics, Johns Hopkins University

"Bob Barbera, in *The Cost of Capitalism,* delivers an excellent recount and puts in perspective the period leading to our current economic condition. Bob's discussion of the economic theory for our current century is stimulating. The book is an excellent read."
—**J. Luther King, Jr.,** CFA, Luther King
Capital Management, Fort Worth, Texas

"This is truly an extraordinarily rare book that should be of great interest to an extremely wide audience from Wall Street practitioners to economics and finance scholars. Using Minskian ideas on financial market crises, Dr. Barbera provides valuable insights on the causes of financial market crises that should be of great use to practitioners on Wall Street At the same time, he provocatively raises numerous questions on the operation of financial markets that cry out for research from scholars in economics and finance."
—**Louis Maccini,** Professor of Economics, Johns Hopkins University

"Bob artfully ties the insights of great economic theorists to the real-life experiences that serious investors confront every day."
—**Tom Marsico,** Chairman, Marsico Capital Management

"Lively and literate, Robert Barbera's *The Cost of Capitalism* translates the economic diagnoses and theories of my father, Hyman Minsky, into language both accessible and entertaining for noneconomists. Barbera constructs a dialogue between household finance and monetary policy while presenting a chronological critique of recent economic events; illustrative anecdotes, both factual and fictive, assure comprehension by a wide audience. Alive with references ranging from Jeffersonian rhetoric to *Casablanca* (and repeatedly back to the Bard), *The Cost of Capitalism* captures the vivacity of a postdinner conversation—not coincidentally my father's favorite forum for elaborating, educating, and entertaining. Barbera presents wisdom distilled through discussion."
—**Diana Minsky,** Art Historian, Bard College

THE COST OF
Capitalism

THE COST OF

Capitalism

Understanding Market Mayhem and
Stabilizing Our Economic Future

Robert J. Barbera

New York   Chicago   San Francisco   Lisbon   London
Madrid   Mexico City   Milan   New Delhi   San Juan
Seoul   Singapore   Sydney   Toronto

The **McGraw·Hill** Companies

1 2 3 4 5 6 7 8 9 0   FGR/FGR   0 1 0 9

ISBN 978-0-07-162844-0
MHID 0-07-162844-4

Figure 4.1 is reproduced by permission from Mark Alan Stamaty.
Figure 14.1 is printed with permission. Illustration by Tom Bachtell, originally published in *The New Yorker*, February 4, 2008.

McGraw-Hill books are available at special quantity discounts to use as premiums and sales promotions, or for use in corporate training programs. To contact a representative, please visit the Contact Us pages at www.mhprofessional.com.

This book is printed on acid-free paper.

To Avis, who somehow after nearly 30 years,
still thinks I am funny

Truth may not depart from human nature.
If what is regarded as truth departs from human nature,
it may not be regarded as truth.
—Confucius, circa 485 BC

CONTENTS

Preface   xi

Acknowledgments   xvii

Chapter | 1   The Postcrisis Case for a New Paradigm   1

Part | I   **Financial Markets and Monetary Policy in Perspective**

Chapter | 2   The Markets Stoke the Boom and Bust Cycle   15

Chapter | 3   The ABCs of Risky Finance   25

Chapter | 4   Financial Markets as a Source of Instability   37

Chapter | 5   Free Market Capitalism: Still the Superior Strategy   55

Chapter | 6   Monetary Policy: Not the Wrong Men, the Wrong Model   71

Part | II   **Economic Experience: 1985-2002**

Chapter | 7   How Financial Instability Emerged in the 1980s   83

Chapter | 8   Financial Mayhem in Asia: Japan's
Implosion and the Asian Contagion   93

Chapter | 9   The Brave-New-World Boom Goes Bust:
The 1990s Technology Bubble   107

Part | III   Emerging Realities: 2007-2008

Chapter | 10   Greenspan's Conundrum Fosters the
Housing Bubble   123

Chapter | 11   Bernanke's Calamity and the Onset
of U.S. Recession   139

Chapter | 12   Domino Defaults, Global Markets Crisis,
and End of the Great Moderation   149

Part | IV   Recasting Economic Theory for the Twenty-First Century

Chapter | 13   Economic Orthodoxy on the Eve of the
Crisis   161

Chapter | 14   Minsky and Monetary Policy   177

Chapter | 15   One Practitioner's Professional Journey   191

Chapter | 16   Global Policy Risks in the Aftermath of
the 2008 Crisis   205

Notes   217

References   225

Index   233

PREFACE

In the winter of 1990, on the eve of the first U.S. war with Iraq, I lunched with a close friend and colleague, Paul DeRosa, a fellow economist. Over the course of the meal I explained that I intended to publish a radical forecast for the U.S. economy. The centerpiece of my outlook was the S&L crisis and the high debt levels of U.S. households. Oil prices and the Mideast, I was convinced, were sideshows. The headline for my research effort was inflammatory. "Cash, at Long, Long Last, Is Trash" was a title meant to put my clients on notice that I expected a wild fall for short-term interest rates and a heady lift for stock and bond prices.

Paul reacted quickly. "Sounds to me," he said, "like vintage Hyman Minsky. Have you run it by him?"

Run it by him? I thought he was dead! Two weeks later, at a dinner at the Mondrian restaurant, Paul and I awaited the man. As a Minsky devotee for some years, I had a fairly rigorous understanding of his theories. I discovered Minsky not in the classroom, but on the job, as a wet-behind-the-ears Wall Street chief economist. I had soon found that conventional economic theory was silent on too many of the big issues I confronted every day. Minsky's analysis came to the rescue. His brilliant insights about the interplay between Wall Street and Main Street had greatly influenced my thinking about markets, economic policy, and the overall economy. But who would Minsky, the man, turn out to be?

With no knowledge whatsoever of Minsky the person, I had unconsciously filled in the blanks. Charles Kindleberger of MIT fame gave Minsky full credit for the theories that drove the famed book *Manias, Panics, and Crashes*. But Kindleberger's personal take on Minsky was hardly complimentary. He labeled Minsky "lugubrious." I married the notion of lugubrious with Minsky's dry writing style and keen attention to detail. The mental image I conjured up looked like the wizened, diminutive actor who portrayed Gandhi, Ben Kingsley.

You can imagine my surprise when Zorba the Greek joined us at our table. Hy was tall, with shocking Einstein hair shooting every which way. He was funny, loud, and mischievous. In short, he was full of life. Conversation began about wine and quickly moved to the worsening credit crisis. I explained, with great trepidation, my sense of how the next few years might unfold. A powerful unwinding of debt excesses, with a historic fall for interest rates, catalyzing first stability and then a massive shift of dollars out of money market funds and into stocks and bonds. The linchpin in the forecast was my call for extraordinary ease by the U.S. Federal Reserve. Overnight interest rates, I ventured, are likely to plunge to 5 percent, a wild ride down from the 8 percent then in place.

"Forget about 5 percent Fed funds," he said. "Tell them 3 percent and you'll be closer to the mark." In the early winter of 1993, Fed funds hit their low for that cycle, touching 3 percent. By that time Hy Minsky and I had become friends, and we chuckled about his superior forecast over lunch.

But in the autumn of 2008 nobody I knew was chuckling. Banks around the world were near insolvency. The U.S. stock market fell by 18 percent in one week—one of its worst weeks ever! By mid-October, Treasury Secretary Hank Paulson held a meeting with the presidents of all major U.S. banks wherein he compelled them to sign documents accepting de facto, partial ownership of their banks by the government. And there were signs of deep economic decline everywhere.

Mainstream thinkers were dumbfounded by the 2008 crisis. In 2007, when troubles began to surface in housing, conventional analysts argued that they would certainly be contained. Monetary policy makers, through much of 2007 and 2008, gave primary attention to rising prices, wildly underestimating the dominolike consequences of plunging U.S. residential real estate. And, quite incredibly, as late as July 2008 a large majority of private economic forecasters continued to argue that the United States would avoid a recession.

Hy Minsky, sadly, died in 1996, and was not around to watch this folly. But I was. Beginning in the early summer of 2007, I began to warn clients of a severe credit crunch, one that would require immediate and aggressive interest rate relief from the Fed. In December 2007, after six months of only modest Fed easing, I warned that recession was baked in the cake, and that the snowballing problems in the financial system would require both dramatic additional Fed ease and some form of direct federal intervention. Just as in 1990, it turned out, my understanding of Hy Minsky's work put me light-years ahead of the consensus thinkers in the months leading up to the 2008 crisis.

But by the summer of 2008, as the world flirted with an economic depression, I decided that simply winning accolades from a select list of my firm's clients was flat out wrong. Hy Minsky's brilliant insights,

I came to believe, needed to be embraced by mainstream economic thinkers. This book, for me, begins that process.

Minsky's thesis can be explained in two sentences:

- A long period of healthy growth convinces people to take bigger and bigger risks.

- When a great many people have made risky bets, small disappointments can have devastating consequences.

For most people, those two notions probably seem fairly obvious. But as I detail in the pages that follow, mainstream policy makers, economists, and central bankers spent the past 25 years willfully denying these two self-evident truths. The global financial crisis of 2008 and the 2008-2009 worldwide recession, this book will make clear, can be laid at the doorstep of these painful omissions of economic fact.

Amidst the wreckage of the recent crisis, calls for expansive retooling of our economic system are building momentum. We witnessed the creation of a succession of new government programs, including the Troubled Asset Recovery Program and the Federal Reserve Board's commercial paper facility. The government insisted that Bear Stearns merge itself out of existence, and the government financed a bailout of AIG. Demands for regulatory overhaul reached a fever pitch. Ben Bernanke acknowledged that the Fed will have to pay more attention to asset markets, including real estate and stock prices. All of these ad hoc responses to our current economic woes make sense. But we must do better.

The Cost of Capitalism makes the case that we all need to think differently about free market capitalism if we want to preserve it. Periodic market mayhem, Minsky taught those who would listen, is a cost we incur for allowing free markets to be in charge of our investment capital. Denying that self-evident truth invites deep economic recession, and in turn discussions of wholesale rejection of free markets. We don't need to abandon our reliance on financial markets, but we do need to come to grips with this flaw. Once policy makers, economists, and investors accept this undeniable reality, we can shape strategies that will reduce both the severity of financial system excesses and the cost, in real economy terms, of financial crises.

As a Wall Street peddler of forecasts, I have a certain ambivalence about championing the Minsky framework. For nearly three decades I have had a competitive edge, relative to conventional analysts, a consequence of my familiarity with Hy's generally ignored diagnoses. But Hyman Minsky dedicated his life to economic study not for his personal gain, but for the public good. On the heels of a year that should generally be recognized as a Minsky crisis, and amid the global recession of 2009 that mainstreamers never saw coming, I feel I owe the memory of my good friend this modest effort.

Robert J. Barbera
January 2009

ACKNOWLEDGMENTS

This is a book that recasts the past 25 years in light of the crisis of 2008. The book argues that evolving economic theory created the framework for policies that ushered in the very tough times that grip the world as the first decade of the new millennium comes to a close. But the book is aimed at economists, investors, *and* the inquisitive general reader. In writing the book, therefore, I struggled to keep it both serious and simple. My strategy to bridge that gulf? I tortured family, friends, and professional and academic colleagues for a good six months as I wrote the text. In other words, I owe an unusually large number of people a big thank you.

The underpinnings of the book evolved over five years, as I taught a course at Johns Hopkins University. I needed to connect the macroeconomics the students were learning to the world that I lived in as a Wall Street forecaster. It turned out to be harder to do than I thought, and my students, since they suffered through my evolution, all deserve a thank you. On that score, Lou Maccini, then the chairman of the Department of Economics at Hopkins, must have felt like he had an extra Ph.D. student, as he provided me with recent literature and commented on early versions of papers that I began to write. Each year, the Levy Institute would invite me to give a paper, and the need to speak to economists about how I thought the system worked—in contrast to what I expected the world to do—also proved useful.

Leah Spiro, my editor at McGraw-Hill, forced my hand. She kept urging me to write the book, and I finally did.

Once the writing commenced I relied on two colleagues much more than should be allowed. Paul DeRosa of Mt. Lucas Partners and Gerry Holtham of Cadwin Partners responded tirelessly to my entreaties for help.

My commentary on the evolution of macroeconomic theory, coming as it does from a practitioner, was rough to be sure. Jon Faust of Johns Hopkins and Charles Weise of Gettysburg College gave many helpful comments on initial drafts.

Jackie Kadre, my business partner for over a decade, and Joann Jacobs, my day-job editor, also worked themselves to the bone to get this book together.

My wife, Avis Barbera, my sister, Susan Barbera, and my eldest son, Michael Barbera, all proved to be invaluable readers. My desire all along was to write this book so that intelligent noneconomists could read it. They cheered when I was succeeding and booed when it seemed impenetrable. I owe each of them a big thank you. I also depended on my sons, Gianni and Nicholas Barbera, for their moral support.

Lastly, I need to tip my hat to Doug Korty. He championed Minsky to me early in my career. And kept telling me to reread it, whenever the world seemed baffling.

As is always the case, I am the only one responsible for the messages in the book. But as good or bad as you perceive them to be, they would be much less good had this large list of folks not helped in the book's creation.

THE COST OF

Capitalism

Chapter | 1

THE POSTCRISIS CASE FOR A NEW PARADIGM

This modern risk-management paradigm held sway for decades.
The whole intellectual edifice, however, collapsed in the summer
of last year.
—Alan Greenspan, Congressional testimony, October 23, 2008

Over the course of 2008, Americans confronted breathtaking Wall Street bankruptcies, unprecedented home foreclosures, and rapid deterioration of the overall economy. In response, a Republican administration engineered the greatest Washington bailout in America's history. Treasury officials, Federal Reserve Board policy makers, and financial market pundits who supported the program tried to justify this massive intrusion by arguing that the crisis reflected unique circumstances that required a temporary relaxation of the time-honored U.S. commitment to free markets. Once the banking system was put back on firm footing, we were told, a dramatic overhaul of regulations would prevent similar upheavals from recurring.

The good news for the global economy is that policy makers worldwide demonstrated in 2008 that they learned the lessons of the 1930s.

When faced with a collapse of the financial system, any and all steps are taken to stabilize the situation. But policies leading up to the crisis of 2008, enacted over the past 25 years, make it abundantly clear that economists, elected officials, and central bankers did not learn the lessons of the 1920s.

The record of the U.S. economy over the past 25 years reveals that financial market crises occurred with painful regularity. To be sure, the mid-1980s through the middle years of this decade were blessed with low inflation, low unemployment, and mild and infrequent recessions. Nonetheless, financial market mayhem was a central feature of the U.S. landscape over that period, notwithstanding the generally healthy picture that was found on Main Street.

Thus, the U.S. economic scorecard leading up to the 2008 crisis invites two questions. Why, amid the relative calm of Main Street, did Wall Street and Washington remain locked in a furious boom and bust cycle? And why did policy makers and mainstream economists, despite decades of obvious evidence to the contrary, willfully ignore the world around them and assert that financial market upheavals were surprising developments?

In *The Cost of Capitalism*, I will argue that market crises are an integral part of our economic system. Capitalist finance, the long sweep of history makes clear, does the best job of allocating the resources of a society. But as can be seen in Figure 1.1, the record also reveals that, with painful regularity, cycles come to an end following errors and excesses that conclude with market upheaval and economic retrenchment.

I will also contend in this book that a confluence of forces over the past 25 years prevented this self-evident truth from being incorporated into the mainstream view. In policy circles the renewed commitment

Figure 1.1

Recurring Financial Crises:
Some Episodes Roiled Stock Markets...
S&P 500 Stock Price Index

Index, Log Scale

Russia's Default

The Burst Technology Bubble

The 1987 Crash

The Housing Debacle and Generalized Market Meltdown

...Others Drove Risky Corporate
Borrowing Rates Sharply Higher
KDP High-Yield Daily Index

Yield (%)

The S&L Crisis

to free market capitalism that took hold, over time, morphed into a willingness to pretend that capitalism is infallible. This overzealous policy maker enthusiasm for purely market solutions coincided with two decades of dominance by free market enthusiasts in economics departments around the world. Mainstream policy makers and academic economists, as a consequence, established a paradigm that denied what centuries of evidence makes clear:

> Late in economic expansions, dubious investments and reckless financing strategies are the central drivers for recessions around the world.

Policy makers refused to accept this reality and ignored explosive trends in financial markets. In particular, both Alan Greenspan and Ben Bernanke cast a blind eye toward breathtaking advances for stocks and credit market instruments during periods of healthy economic growth. And the entire complex of Washington regulators allowed Wall Street investment houses to garner an enormous share of global banking business despite the fact that these institutions had no legal access to the safety nets put in place for commercial banks in the aftermath of the Great Depression. It is not hyperbole, therefore, to lay the multi-trillion-dollar bill for the 2008 financial system bailout, and the deep recession of 2008-2009, at the doorstep of misguided confidence in the infallibility of free markets.

Is this book, therefore, simply an indictment of Alan Greenspan and Ben Bernanke? Absolutely not! It is not that we put our trust in the wrong people, but that we embraced the wrong paradigm. Going forward, both policy makers and mainstream economic thinkers need to embrace a model for capitalism that squares with both its virtues and its flaws. The events of 2008 revealed that using simple-minded free market rhetoric as a policy guide is a recipe for disaster.

At the same time, however, the ravages of the 2008 crisis do not justify a violent leftward lurch. Risk takers are the main drivers in the free market machinery. Their efforts go a long way toward explaining the lofty growth rates capitalist economies have delivered in the postwar years. Rather, an enlightened synthesis, one that celebrates free market risk taking but establishes policies to rein in inevitable excesses, needs to be forged. In *The Cost of Capitalism*, I attempt to begin a dialogue on this crucial issue.

Serenity on Main Street and the Boom and Bust Cycle of the Past 25 Years

In years to come a casual reader of economic history may find it hard to piece together how things so quickly went from serenity to panic as the first decade of the new millennium came to a close. Paradoxically, the seeds of the 2008 crisis can be found in the widespread acceptance of the notion that the U.S. economy, over the previous decades, had taken a major turn for the better.

Clearly, traditional measures of economic health justified an optimistic bent. Following the dismal economic performance of the 1970s, the United States tallied up an impressive list of economic successes. In the 1960s and 1970s, inflation and unemployment climbed irregularly to unprecedented heights. Recessions were frequent and deep. In stark contrast, from the early 1980s through 2006, inflation, unemployment, and output changes were much less violent. Dubbed the "Great Moderation" in economic circles and the "Goldilocks economy" on Wall Street—for its not-too-hot, not-too-cold perfection—this improved snapshot was generally regarded as a triumph for U.S. monetary policy.

But the long list of financial market crises that dotted the landscape of the past 25 years make it clear that reduced volatility for the U.S.

economy did not reduce wild Wall Street swings. In succession, we witnessed the 1987 stock market crash, the S&L crisis of the early 1990s, the Long-Term Capital Management meltdown, and the spectacular technology boom and bust dynamic of the late nineties. In Asia we had two bouts of financial market mayhem: Japan's early 1990 collapse (see Figure 1.2) which was followed a few years later by the panic that swept through much of the newly emerging Asian economies.

As it turned out, this daunting list of financial market upheavals were simply dress rehearsals for what was to later occur. The unprecedented rise and then swoon in U.S. residential real estate catalyzed a global financial market meltdown of unprecedented proportions. And the cost around the world includes a deep global recession. Any notion that the Great Moderation was a permanent fixture died in 2008.

Figure 1.2

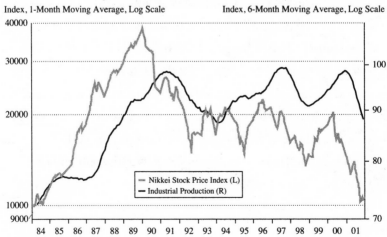

**Japan's Stock Market Collapse and
the Lost Decade for Its Economy**
Japan: Nikkei Stock Market Index vs. Industrial Production

How did things go from so good to so bad in such short order? Mayhem on Wall Street following serenity on Main Street, I contend, is no coincidence. Instead, quiescence on Main Street invites big risk taking on Wall Street. And big wagers create the potential for big problems from small disappointments—despite the reality of a moderate economic backdrop. And therein lies the paradox. Goldilocks growth on Main Street spawned risky finance on Wall Street and, ultimately, the crisis of 2008.

Mainstream economists missed this dynamic because they were so excited about low wage and price inflation. Thus, a legion of conventional analysts simply failed to recognize that the inflationary boom and bust cycle of the 1970s had been replaced by an equally violent Wall Street driven cycle.

Hyman Minsky, a renegade financial economist of the postwar period, would be amused if he were alive today. Minsky, throughout his professional life, insisted that finance was always the key force for mayhem in capitalist economies. He put it this way:

> Whenever full employment is achieved and sustained, businessmen and bankers, heartened by success, tend to accept larger doses of debt financing. During periods of tranquil expansion, profit-seeking financial institutions invent and reinvent "new" forms of money, substitutes for money in portfolios, and financing techniques for various types of activity: financial innovation is a characteristic of our economy in good times.[1]

Minsky argued that this phenomenon guaranteed financial instability. He developed a thesis that linked the boom and bust cycle to the way in which investment is bankrolled. He made two simple observations. First, the persistence of benign real economy circumstance invites belief in its permanence. Second, growing confidence invites riskier finance. Minsky combined these two insights and asserted that boom and bust business cycles were inescapable in a free market economy—*even if central bankers were able to tame big swings for inflation.*

Much of this book critically reexamines the last several decades with an eye toward the interplay of Goldilocks growth expectations versus increasingly risky finance. I make the case that U.S. recessions in 1990, 2001, and 2008 all reflected violent swings in attitudes about investment—and the financing of that investment. Likewise the rise and collapse of Japan Inc. and the boom and swoon for emerging Asian economies in the late 1990s followed a pattern perfectly consistent with our investment/financing-focused model.

The Cost of Capitalism will also investigate a second question. If a model centered on investment finance is such a great guide, why did such theories remain on the periphery of both policy and mainstream economic circles?

On that score I identify three forces that prevented this paradigm from breaking into the mainstream of economic thought. Most important, the Reagan revolution followed by the collapse of the former Soviet empire combined to produce a global embrace and celebration of free market ideology. The celebration was justified. Free markets are *the best* strategy available to provide for a population's economic needs. Over time, however, the enthusiasm morphed into a misguided notion—that free market outcomes are *the perfect* strategy and, therefore, cannot be improved upon through governmental action. Thus, belief in Adam Smith's "invisible hand" gave way to enthusiasm for the market's "infallible hand."

In addition, in academia a select group of high-powered mathematicians, with decidedly conservative biases, built models dedicated to the proposition that the market always gets it right. The constructs were underpinned by the assumption that people are well-informed and act rationally. As the architecture tied to rational expectations became more and more embedded and elaborate, it became harder and harder to focus on how the real world operated. Thus, a generation of brilliant economic theoreticians developed and expanded upon theories that were increasingly at odds with the world around them.

More to the point, the models denied certain key self-evident truths. They failed to acknowledge that financial markets periodically go haywire. They failed to link market upheavals with boom and bust cycles. And as a consequence they led their creators to assert, incorrectly, that there was no theoretical justification for the visible hand of government to come to the rescue of banks and other financial institutions.

Finally, the marginalization of Minsky also clearly reflects Minsky's radical policy recommendations and the embrace of these decidedly left-wing directives by his academic followers. A large majority of Americans, including this author, categorically rejects Minsky's call for socialized investment.

But it makes no sense to ignore the Minsky diagnosis. Not in order to sound unequivocally committed to free markets. Not in order to legitimize your mathematical models. And certainly not to simply make sure no one suspects you of being an advocate of left-wing solutions. The model explains the past 25 years in a way that conventional analysis does not. It makes it clear that there was no escaping a mega bailout in 2008. Now, amid the wreckage of the 2008 crisis, with the Great Moderation dead, policy makers, business leaders, and investors need to come to understand the insights of Hyman Minsky.

Coming to Terms with the 2008 Global Capital Markets Crisis

Investors, business leaders, policy makers, and economists are right to champion free market capitalism and celebrate moderate inflation. Schumpeter was right. Entrepreneurs in a capitalist system are the engine of growth. On Main Street we embrace his concept of creative destruction as the price of progress. But his Ph.D. student, Hy Minsky, also had key insights. Dubious finance and market mayhem define the last scenes of modern day cycles. Periodically we are forced to collapse interest rates and shore up the banking system. Simply put, it is a cost we incur for embracing capitalism.

Monetary policy needs to be conducted with an understanding that modern day excesses are at least as likely to begin in asset markets as they are likely to arise from inflationary wage settlements. Ignoring improbable market gains and dubious credit finance on the grounds that "the Fed can't outguess the market" is a strategy that all but assures the need for breathtaking bailouts.

I recognize that my call for central banks to lean against the winds of financial market sentiment sounds like heresy to doctrinaire free market boosters. But the 2008 financial crisis, and the global retrenchment that it spawned, is giving new life to much more radical recommendations. Governments now own a piece of the world's banking system. The risk is that this becomes the general state of affairs. I believe that a move toward the socialization of investment—again, a solution Minsky himself endorsed—would amount to throwing the baby out with the bathwater.

To build a consensus around an expanded role for central bankers, we need mainstream academic economists to retrain their sights on the world around them. They need to provide a more realistic foundation for thinking about economic questions, including and especially pertaining to monetary policy guidelines. To do this they must end their willful disregard for the increasingly prominent role that finance plays in modern day boom and bust cycles. And they will have to put aside models that assume people are well-informed and always act rationally.

In summation, the events of 2008 make clear that economic policy and the theories that buttress policy are in need of a new paradigm. While we celebrate the virtues of capitalism, we need to come to terms with its obvious flaws. Acknowledging that asset market excesses and dubious finance play central roles in modern day cycles is the critical step we must take in order to design a winning strategy for the twenty-first century.

Part | I

FINANCIAL MARKETS AND MONETARY POLICY IN PERSPECTIVE

Chapter | 2

THE MARKETS STOKE THE BOOM AND BUST CYCLE

It is a joke in Britain to say that the War Office
is always preparing for the last war.
—Winston Churchill, *The Gathering Storm*, 1945-1953

Over the past 25, years policy makers, Wall Street pundits, and mainstream academic economists joined together in a celebration of the Goldilocks economy. With the dismal record of the 1970s as their point of comparison, mainstream analysts focused on the not-too-hot, not-too-cold economic backdrop that over time produced sharp declines for both inflation and unemployment. They were excited about the fact that recessions—outright declines for the economy—were rare and mild. And they concluded that this Great Moderation was a triumph for monetary policy. Federal Reserve Board policy makers, by adjusting interest rates to keep inflation at bay, had vanquished the brutal boom and bust cycles that gripped the U.S. economy in the 1960s and 1970s. And the payoff was significant. From 1983 through 2007 the U.S. economy was blessed with limited inflation, low unemployment, and healthy economic growth.

But policy makers and mainstream analysts shared two critical blind spots that clouded their thinking about the last several decades. They confused keeping wage and price pressures moderate with keeping the economy free of excesses. And they viewed financial crises and Washington bailouts, when they were needed, as singular one-off events. Somehow these crises were independent from the generally healthy backdrop they could point to before the serious recession of 2008 arrived. These two analytical flaws evolved in large part because mainstream thinkers continued to fight the last war: the war against inflation.

Vanquishing the Boom and Bust Cycle of the Sixties and Seventies . . .

When Paul Volcker was appointed chairman of the Federal Reserve Board in 1979, the United States was in the late stages of a frightening explosion of inflation. Volcker confronted a nation that had surrendered to the notion that inflation was destined to worsen as the years went by. Labor unions, in an attempt to protect their rank and file, had wrestled cost of living adjustments from management. Social security payments were indexed to inflation. Thus, developments that led to rising prices almost automatically would elicit a leap in wage payments. And once higher wages raised company costs, companies would raise prices again. By the late 1970s this wage-price spiral looked to be nearly unstoppable.

Volcker thought otherwise. He was convinced that a steadfast commitment to stable prices by the U.S. Federal Reserve Board could break the back of this entrenched inflation. The costs would clearly be high. But Volcker knew that the political will to break inflation was firmly in place. Indeed, in the end it took back-to-back recessions and a spectacular rise in unemployment, which peaked at 10.8 percent in 1982. By the mid-1970s, U.S. consumer sentiment surveys rated inflation, not unemployment, the number one economic problem. Volcker put U.S. monetary policy on a path designed to eradicate inflation and it worked. By mid-1985, when he left office, year-on-year gains for inflation were running in low single digits, dramatically below the 13 percent inflation rate in place shortly after he took office in 1979.

When looked at through the prism of the Volcker challenge, the Greenspan years (1987-2006) are nothing short of spectacular. Inflation fell to near zero, and averaged only 3 percent for the period. The jobless rate fell below 4 percent, and averaged 5.6 percent, well below its lofty level of the 1970s. Over the period, economic growth was generally healthy. There were only two recessions recorded, and by historic standards both were short and shallow, as can be seen in Figures 2.1 and 2.2. Inflation, for all intents and purposes, had been vanquished. And the swings for the overall economy were much tamer. Call it what you will, this Great Moderation or Goldilocks economy was a vast improvement over the Great Inflation of the 1960-1970 period.

Figure 2.1

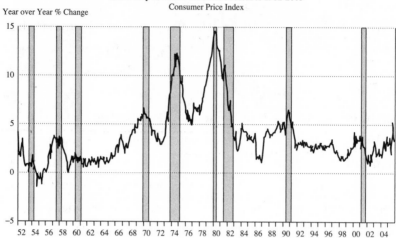

**The Great Inflation of the 1960s-1970s
Gave Way to Moderate Price Pressures 1982-2005**
Consumer Price Index

Year over Year % Change

Figure 2.2

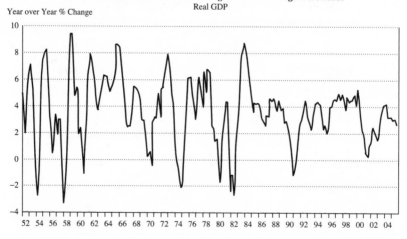

**From the 1950s through the Early 1980s the Boom and Bust Cycle
Was Violent. From Mid-1985 through Mid-2005 Swings Were Mild.**
Real GDP

Year over Year % Change

... But Failing to Recognize the Emerging Cycle as the New Millennium Approached

Thus, spikes for prices that drive labor costs sharply higher, leading to deep and protracted recessions, disappeared from the U.S. economic landscape over the past several decades. But the notion that excesses leading to economic turmoil were largely things of the past was wrong. Conventional thinkers, as they celebrated the Goldilocks backdrop, were watching the wrong movie. Significantly, at the U.S. Federal Reserve Board, both Alan Greenspan and his successor, Ben Bernanke, were self-satisfied about the world they confronted, *because they were fighting the last war.* Their vision was based on a nearsighted perspective: the belief that the most dangerous threat to our economic stability was allowing the inflation monster to get out of control, leading inevitably to crackdown and recession.

That scenario lost its currency in the 1980s. The last five major global cyclical events were the early 1990s recession—largely occasioned by the U.S. Savings & Loan crisis, the collapse of Japan Inc. after the stock market crash of 1990, the Asian crisis of the mid-1990s, the fabulous technology boom/bust cycle at the turn of the millennium, and the unprecedented rise and then collapse for U.S. residential real estate in 2007-2008. All five episodes delivered recessions, either global or regional. In no case was there a significant prior acceleration of wages and general prices. In each case, an investment boom and an associated asset market ran to improbable heights and then collapsed. From 1945 to 1985 there was no recession caused by the instability of investment prompted by financial speculation—and since 1985 there has been no recession that has not been caused by these factors.

Surging asset prices amid increasingly dubious finance define excess in the modern day cycle. Wall Street, in each of the past three U.S. cycles, designed its way into hyperrisky territory. When Federal Reserve Board policy makers raised rates, responding to wage and price issues, mayhem in the world of finance both precipitated recessions and required breathtaking bouts of Fed ease—and in two cases unprecedented government bailouts. Thus, the Fed's focus on wages and prices permitted excesses to run to great heights, and the aftermath required a Fed and government response that seemed inexplicably large to those focused on the mild cycles for wages and prices.

In 1990-1991, following the spike of oil prices induced by the first Iraq war, the Fed raised rates and recession ensued. When the war ended, oil prices plunged and inflation worries receded. Alan Greenspan, in the spring of 1991, speculated that the fall of oil prices and the consequent jump for consumer purchasing power could well ignite a vibrant recovery. Within a year he was singing a very different tune. "Secular headwinds" associated with the worsening S&L crisis and heavy problems for banks and consumers, he explained, likely would consign the U.S. economy to a multiyear period of subpar growth.

At the White House Conference on the New Economy, in the spring of 2000, President Bill Clinton championed the boom in technology investment, anticipating bright prospects for a Golden Era. Rising energy prices, however, had given Fed policy makers the green light to tighten interest rates somewhat more aggressively. Within a year, Federal Reserve Board concerns about inflation were, incredibly, replaced by worries about deflation—a generalized and unhealthy fall for prices. Collapsing technology share prices, it turned out, had led to widespread cutbacks in technology activity and a plethora of bankruptcies for technology start-up companies. By early 2003 the overnight interest rate controlled by the Fed had been driven to 1 percent! Ben Bernanke, who was vice chairman at the time, explained that Fed policy could keep providing stimulus, even if it took the rate to zero: we can buy bonds and drive long rates lower, he explained prophetically.

Finally, in 2005 soon-to-retire Alan Greenspan coined a term to express his puzzlement about interest rate dynamics in the United States. He labeled the failure of long-term interest rates to rise— despite a succession of Fed-engineered interest rate increases—a "conundrum." But Greenspan chose to label the problem instead of respond to it. Pointing to tame core inflation and moderate wage gains, he justified the slow move up for Fed funds and accepted the easy interest rate backdrop that persisted. The resultant run-up for housing starts and the climb in house prices were unprecedented.

The Fed's engineered short-term rate increases were finally met by rising long rates in 2006. The consequent fall for home prices and housing activity exceeded any downturns witnessed in the United States since the Great Depression. The Fed began to ease, in the fall of 2007. And as we have now witnessed, by the fall of 2008 the most expansive government bailout in history was being deployed in an effort to rescue the financial system. And the Great Moderation ended with a hefty global recession.

Common Threads of the Last Three Cycles

What are the central dynamics of the past three U.S. recessions? Conventional wisdom, in each case, embraced the notion that a healthy overall backdrop and a vigilant Federal Reserve Board promised blue skies ahead. Triumph against the Great Inflation instilled confidence in an extended expansion in the latter half of the 1980s. The early 1990s confidence in a Goldilocks not-too-hot, not-too-cold economy gave way to enthusiasm about a "brave new world" of inflation-free, technology-driven boom. In the years leading up to the 2008 recession, China, India, and other emerging market booms promised a long-term run for global growth.

Wall Street investment banks, with confidence in healthy economywide fundamentals, designed and championed new financial instruments. The late 1980s brought us junk bonds. The late 1990s witnessed the spectacular dot-com IPO market. And wizardry in the first cycle of this century gave explosive rise to the offering and use of subprime mortgages.

Throughout these periods, the U.S. Federal Reserve Board policy makers insisted that inflation was the only excess under their purview. Their focus on tame wage and price pressures, in each instance, guided money policy for extended periods. When Fed policy was tightened, in response to some lift for inflation, the collateral damage on Wall Street shocked policy makers. The scope of Fed ease in response to Wall Street/financial system crises was breathtaking. In two of three cases, the late 1980s and the 2008 crises, major Washington bailouts were also required to stabilize the banking system.

 The evidence is clear. Asset markets are not a sideshow now, but the main engines of cycles. Monetary authorities cannot contribute to stabilizing the economy by ignoring financial markets. If equity markets and real estate markets are rising significantly faster than any trend that can be justified without excessive ingenuity, and credit is growing quickly, then interest rates are too low, whatever general inflation may be doing. When the markets start to fall and credit contracts, it is not the time to dream of punishing the guilty. Central banks must overcome their squeamishness, incorporate asset prices in their definition of stability, and thereby have a say about asset prices on the way up as well as on the way down.

In summation, the past three economic cycles have been driven by Wall Street finance. The violence of the reversals on Wall Street and the spectacular need for Washington rescue in part reflect misguided fascination with modest wage and price pressures. Simply put, Federal Reserve Board policy makers need to expand their definition of excess if they want do better going forward.

Chapter | 3

THE ABCs OF RISKY FINANCE

The fault, dear Brutus, lies not in our stars,
But in ourselves.

—William Shakespeare, *Julius Caesar*

If you never understood why the A tranch of a collateralized mort-gage obligation was supposed to be nearly risk free, relax. It turns out that their rocket scientist inventors didn't understand them either. What we now know is that high-powered mathematical screw-ups tied to slicing and dicing mortgages were awe-inspiring. Indeed, it is not an overstatement to say that flawed mortgage-backed paper precipi-tated the banking crisis of 2007-2008. For our purposes, these rocket scientists can be dismissed with a quip from Warren Buffett: "Beware of geeks bearing formulas."[1]

That said, getting a handle on the basic concepts of risky finance is essential. The good news is that it is easy to do. Once you get the fundamentals down, you will see that the sophisticated financial architecture invented over the past few decades, though impenetra-ble piece by piece, in its entirety is nothing more than artifice. Risk can be divvied up and sold to willing buyers. But you can't make it go away.

Given the extraordinary carnage witnessed in the U.S. housing market over the past several years, the simplest way to get a grip on risky finance is to jump into the now treacherous world of getting a mortgage to buy your first home. Simply by following two fictional home buyers through their first few years of home ownership, we can learn about fear versus greed. We can get a basic understanding of *financial leverage*, the importance of monthly *cash flows*, and the concept of *margin of safety*. Most important, we will see, in full color, the upside and the downside to prudent versus risky investing.

Hanna and Hal Each Buy a First House

Twins in their early 20s graduate from Johns Hopkins University and land good jobs in the Baltimore area. Mom, a successful obstetrician, rewards them each for their efforts with a $50,000 graduation present. She suggests that they use their newfound wealth as a down payment on a house. She also delivers some time-honored advice. She suggests that their home purchases should be linked to their incomes. A good rule of thumb, she explains, is to put at least 15 percent down and to have monthly mortgage payments that do not exceed one-third of after-tax income. "Remember *first, do no harm.* Buy a house to start yourself on a good road, but don't stretch yourself too thin."

Hal gets out a calculator and quickly figures out the house he can afford, given the money and the advice he got from Mom. If he buys a $300,000 house, he will be able to put $45,000 down, 15 percent of the house price. He qualifies, at his local bank, for a 30-year fixed rate mortgage, with a 6 percent interest rate. A $255,000 mortgage at 6 percent translates to roughly a $1,529 monthly mortgage payment.

Hal's gross income is $80,000 per year, leaving him with around $4,800 per month after taxes. That means his $1,529 monthly payment will be a bit below one-third of his available monthly cash, right in line with Mom's rule of thumb. He finds and purchases a $300,000 house.

Hanna, Hal's adventurous twin, has a much bolder plan. Like her brother, she has a job that pays $80,000. She has similar living expenses. And Mom gave her $50,000 as well. But she has a very different attitude toward *risk and reward*. Hanna knows that home values have risen 10 percent per year in her neighborhood of choice in each of the past five years. Furthermore, she learned from a friend at an investment bank that median home prices in the United States went up in every year since 1966, when the National Association of Realtors began to track these statistics (see Figure 3.1). Finally, Hanna understands that "to make a lot of money you have to risk some money." In economic phraseology, she understands the concept of leverage!

Hanna recognizes that she will see some modest improvement in her economic circumstances if she mirrors her brother's plan. But she dreams about a house with a view of the Chesapeake Bay. Why not bank on rising house prices and buy a much bigger house? She spends three days furiously crunching numbers. And then she cackles, "I've got it! I've divined a strategy that will put me in twice the house of my slow-witted brother. And what's more, in a few years' time I'll be on my way to riches, and he'll be frozen in his middle-class existence!"

Figure 3.1

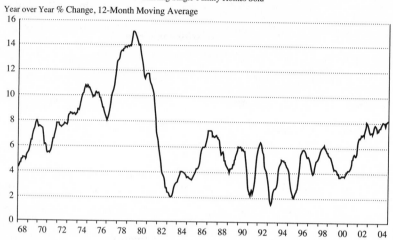

**Median House Prices: In Positive Territory,
without Exception, from 1966 through 2004**
National Association of Realtors: Median Sales Price,
Existing Single-Family Homes Sold

What did Hanna decide to do? Here's how she explained her brainstorm to a friend:

> I will only put a small amount down on my house. I will keep the rest of Mom's gift in the bank so I can use it to help make the mortgage payments on a house that my income can't cover. Moreover, I'll get a teaser rate loan, one that has a low interest rate for two years. Before I run out of Mom's cash, I'll refinance. When I refinance, I will increase my loan, so as to take more cash out. The money I take out will cover the big prepayment penalty that my teaser loan carries. And it will give me the cash I need to meet the next two years' worth of monthly mortgage payments.

Hanna proceeds to buy a house for $600,000, twice the price of Hal's modest home. She puts only 2 percent down, versus Hal's 15 percent. She gets a 2-28 subprime loan, where you pay a low rate for two years, then a high rate for 28 years. In two years' time she intends to refinance. She will increase the size of her loan by $50,000. That sum will provide her with the cash for her prepayment penalty, and the rest will help pay the next two years' worth of mortgage payments.

Hanna is ecstatic about her strategy. In six years' time, if all goes according to plan, her house will be worth $1 million. She will only owe $600,000. Then she will be able to sell the house and move to L.A. with nearly half a million dollars in her back pocket.

And what makes it all the more delicious to her? Twin brother Hal will be left in the slow lane. Hal will have lived in a starter home for six years. He will still owe his bank $225,000, leaving him with equity of only $150,000. So she will have lived high on the hog and walked away with more than twice the dough. Life can be grand, if you know how to play the angles.

A Dream Come True, or Tears and a Journey?

What happens to Hanna and Hal? That depends critically on one thing. When did they buy their houses? If our Hanna/Hal saga began in 2000, things will have worked like a charm for the leveraged twin. Hanna would have been able to sell her home in 2006, after two rounds of successful refinancing, and flown first class to the Left Coast. Brother Hal would have been left in the dust. If, however, Hanna hatched her plan in 2006, all would have been lost for her in the first two years of its existence.

That is, of course, because of what happened to house prices. From 2000 to 2006 they rose by nearly 10 percent per year, matching Hanna's expectations. But from 2006 to 2008 they fell, in some places violently. What happens if they fall? Let's replay the movie. House prices, bucking history, fall 5 percent in both 2006 and 2007. How do Hal and Hanna fare?

When a comparable home sells for $270,000 a few blocks away, Hal suffers a pang of remorse about his $300,000 purchase. He still owes around $250,000 on the house. If he sold today, he'd walk away with roughly $20,000. So his equity—the part of the home's value over and above the loan he has on the home—is now down to only $20,000, well below its original $45,000 level when he bought the house. He calls Mom. She advises him to relax, tells him that things can go up and down over the short term, but if he pays his mortgage and enjoys his nice new home, things will work out just fine. Hal has a beer and puts on the Ravens game.

Hanna, in stark contrast, is filing for bankruptcy. She kept tabs on home resales in her neighborhood—that is, until it became too painful to do so. She was told by her bankruptcy lawyer that his best guess was that her $600,000 home would only fetch $538,000 in the depressed market of 2009. That completely wipes out both her equity and her vision of joining the leisure class. More important, she faces an immediate crisis: she has no way to get cash to stay in the house. The fact that her house is now worth $50,000 less than her mortgage eliminates any chance for her to refinance. That means she cannot prevent the sharp jump in interest payments that are slated to occur with her 2-28 loan. What is worse, even the new government program that would freeze her payments at the teaser rate is of no use to her. Hanna's plan required refinancing to extract cash from her appreciating home value. Without the extra money from the climbing house price, her $80,000 a year salary simply cannot support a mortgage of nearly $600,000. Hanna defaults on her home and takes the Greyhound bus to Phoenix (see Table 3.1).

Table 3.1

	Hal	Hanna
Cash From Mom	$50,000.0	$50,000.0
House Price	$300,000.0	$600,000.0
% Downpayment	15.0%	2.0%
Downpayment Amount	$45,000.0	$12,000.0
Loan Amount	$255,000.0	$588,000.0
Starting Equity Value	$45,000.0	$12,000.0
Cash Less Downpayment	$5,000.0	$38,000.0
Yearly Income	$80,000.0	$80,000.0
Tax Rate	28.0%	28.0%
Post Tax Income	$57,600.0	$57,600.0
Monthly Post Tax Income	$4,800.0	$4,800.0
Mortgage Details		
Type	30yr Fixed	2-28 Interest Only
Mortgage Rate	6%	5% Interest Only For 2 Yrs
Monthly Mortgage Payment	$1,528.9	$2,450.0
Mtg Payment/Monthly Income	31.9%	51.0%
Mortgage Rate		7% Fully Amortized After 2 years
Monthly Mortgage Payment		$3,996.0
Mtg Payment/Monthly Income		83.3%
% House Appreciation/(Depreciation)	(10.0%)	(10.0%)
House Value	$270,000.0	$540,000.0
Loan Amount	255,000.0	588,000.0
Equity Value Post Price Decline	$15,000.0	($48,000.0)
Comment		Can't Afford Higher Rate After 2 yrs. Hanna would have to write a check for ~$48K (which she doesn't have) to bank to refinance.
End Game	Keeps paying mortgage despite drop in value of house.	House Foreclosed upon.

Minsky's Insights on Debt and Risk

There are two lessons from the saga of Hal and Hanna. If things go according to plan, the more debt you use, the more magnified your gains. Conversely, if things go awry, the larger the cushion you have, the more likely you are to avoid bankruptcy.

Hal, by listening to Mom, established financial arrangements that provided for a healthy margin of safety. Hanna, after consulting with an investment banker about house price trends, designed a financial scheme that held out the promise of much higher returns.

But the key insight to gain from this long-winded anecdote is not that it pays to listen to Mom! Instead, we need to think about how people, over the course of an economic expansion, change their attitudes about risk taking. By 2008 everybody *knew* that it was critically important to have a margin of safety in place when buying a house. But in 2006, no fewer than four bestselling books were published celebrating some version of Hanna's leveraged real estate investment strategy.

Minsky's financial instability hypothesis depends critically on what amounts to a sociological insight. People change their minds about taking risks. They don't make a onetime rational judgment about debt use and stock market exposure and stick to it. Instead, they change their minds over time. And history is quite clear about how they change their minds. The longer the good times endure, the more people begin to see wisdom in risky strategies like Hanna's.

Minsky's second observation extends directly from the first. When a large number of people have put a risky strategy into place, *small disappointments can have devastating consequences.*

Think back to Hanna and Hal. House prices, in the second scenario, fell by 5 percent a year in 2007 and 2008. After rising for

50 years, and on the heels of a doubling over the previous 15 years, a two-year 10 percent pullback should have been a nonevent for borrowers, lenders, and the overall economy. After all, we didn't say that housing prices plunged. They simply slipped back to levels in place in 2005.

If the vast majority of homeowners had followed Hal's lead, the pullback is ignored. But Hanna is highly leveraged. She needs her house price to keep rising simply to pay her mortgage. Thus a small fall for the house price and Hanna is in foreclosure.

When the vast majority of home buyers adopt Hanna's plan—as was true in California, Florida, Nevada, and Arizona—foreclosures abound. Once foreclosures become widespread, banks are stuck with a rapidly growing number of houses they have to sell. Then home prices begin to fall much more steeply. But it is important to recognize that Hanna's risky finance strategy set the economy on its downward path *as soon as house prices fell by a smidgeon*. Minsky's thesis makes it clear that small disappointments generate violent destabilizing consequences when risky finance is the rule. The 2007 downturn for housing, the financial crisis, and the painful 2008-2009 recession are all of a piece. And they started with widespread willingness to embrace risky finance.

The Minsky Moment and Walking Bankrupts

Hanna's plight teaches us about the need to have cash inflows that match monthly cash payments. But once Hanna and her like-minded brethren hit the skids, we discover that a good part of the crisis associated with the Hanna plan is not Hanna's problem—it's the bank's problem.

Recall that when Hanna boarded the bus for Phoenix, she had handed her house to her bank. The bank, at that moment, had a house that it could sell for $538,000. But it loaned Hanna $588,000. Thus, the bank lost $50,000 on the deal. Banks are in the business of borrowing money from some and lending to others. The value of what they owe—their liabilities—is always supposed to be lower than the value of what is owed to them—their assets. When they subtract their liabilities from their assets, the remainder is their equity.

The problem for banks arises if the banks have lots of Hannalike loans in their portfolio. As the pie charts in Figure 3.2 make clear, that is exactly what happened. In 2001 nearly 60 percent of mortgage borrowers looked like Hal, and less than 10 percent were involved in risky finance. By 2006 fully one-third of home buyers opted for risky mortgage products. Moreover, a large number of homeowners with no moving plans decided that Hanna had the right strategy. If we combine refinancing with risky home buying finance, we discover that by 2006, nearly half of the housing-related financing was done with risky loans.

When the bank forecloses, it replaces one asset with another. The loan to Hanna is replaced by the house, since the loan has gone bust and the bank now owns the home. But the loan was for $588,000, and the house is worth $538,000. If lots of home loans go the way of Hanna's loan, then the total value of the bank's assets falls below the total value of its loans to other people—its liabilities.

When a bank's liabilities are larger than its assets, it is bankrupt. When banks, and investors in those banks, simultaneously *discover* that bank assets are worth much less than previously thought, we have hit the Minsky moment. At that juncture, if we force banks to

Figure 3.2

Risky Finance in Mortgages

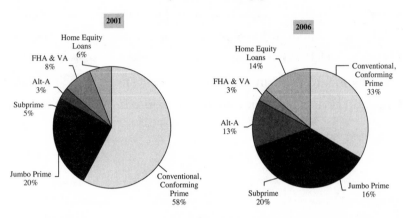

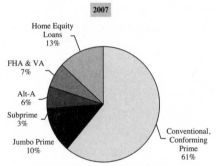

Source: Inside Mortgage Finance (by dollar amount); 2007 data is as of December 31, 2007

revalue their assets to current market prices, it becomes apparent that they are insolvent. At such moments, Minsky liked to talk about the "parade of walking bankrupts" that dotted the banking community landscape.

But we don't drive all banks into bankruptcy. We collapse interest rates. We engineer forced mergers. We come to the banks' rescue with expensive bailouts. Policy makers, thankfully, learned their lessons from the 1930s. There is a paper trail of furious governmental efforts, cycle to cycle, each aimed at protecting the banking system.

The most important two lessons to take away from the saga of Hanna and Hal? When good times persist, risky finance is the logical outcome. Risky finance, in turn, sets both the borrower and the lender up for mayhem somewhere down the road.

Chapter | 4

FINANCIAL MARKETS AS A SOURCE OF INSTABILITY

Those of us who looked to the self-interest of lending institutions to protect shareholder's equity (myself especially) are in a state of shocked disbelief.

—Alan Greenspan testimony, October 23, 2008

I'm shocked, shocked to find that gambling is going on in here!

—Captain Louis Renault, as played by Claude Raines, *Casablanca*, 1942

Simply by following the actions of two home buyers we were able to get a glimpse of the way more accepting attitudes toward risk play a central role in the boom and bust cycle of an economy. Now consider the issues of risk appetites and cycles from an economywide perspective. Begin by inventing a population of well-informed and rational investors living in a world that has business cycles. We discover that their approach to investing has no relation to the habits of investors in the real world.

Why does our world conflict with the well-informed and rational universe? First off because in the real world the future is unknowable.

And in the real world, people go off the deep end, with painful regularity. Our framework for thinking about risk and the economy, therefore, has as its centerpiece what Hy Minsky called "pervasive uncertainty." More simply, when it comes to the future, *nobody knows!* How do they guess? It turns out that Yesterday informs opinion about Tomorrow. And when we string together a succession of happy yesterdays, confidence in a happy tomorrow builds and risk taking flourishes.

We learned from Hanna that risky finance sets a person up for tragic consequences from small disappointments. In this chapter we confirm that what was true for Hanna is also an economywide truth.

The Rational Inhabitants of Never Never Land

Imagine a world free of banks and Wall Street. When people spend less than they earn, they hand their savings over directly to companies. The companies use the proceeds to invest in new production facilities. What could go wrong? Swings in consumer saving, it turns out, don't square well with company needs to pay for big investment projects.[1] This periodic mismatch between saving and investing has a big influence on the number of investment projects built and the timing of the investment.[2]

The clustering of investment opportunities and their interaction with saving can easily produce a boom and bust cycle. But the cycle is not totally regular: enough play exists in both savings and investment schedules to eliminate all chance of perfect prediction.[3] Nonetheless, with some consistency, this economy exhibits a boom and bust pattern—broadly seven to ten years of expansion followed by one to two years of pause or decline.

Now let's introduce a financial system to this world. Let's suppose that stock and bond markets provide a means for businesses to borrow and households to lend. Let's suppose further that the world is peopled with 24/7 rational thinkers, and that these rational agents over time figure out the general pattern of the investment cycle that defines their world. In this Never Never Land, how would the ups and downs of the financial world compare with the real economy boom and bust cycle?

Financiers, we are supposing, recognize that their economy has an unmistakable boom and bust cycle. Armed with this enlightened view, money men and women would try to protect themselves from this boom and bust pattern. How? They would step back from risky lending when an expansion had been going for some years—with the knowledge that recession was sooner or later inevitable. Conversely, early in recoveries they would recommit to risky finance, with the confidence that the next recession was quite a few years down the road. In Wall Street parlance, investors would be bullish early in expansions and become progressively more bearish as the uptrend unfolded.

The simple fairy tale we just described depicts a world of rational financiers, each blessed with a basic understanding of what the future will bring. Thus Never Never Landers are able to prudently facilitate financial transactions. And because they lend more stringently as recessions approach, and more generously as recoveries begin, their insights moderate the swings in the real economy. They are, in short, a stabilizing force.

There are two problems with this fairy tale. First, there never has been a cycle in which economic players are blessed with a basic idea of what the future will bring. And second, there has never been a cycle that was free of false confidences and flights of fancy from financiers, lenders, and borrowers. Instead, in the real world, financial market swings—at business cycle turning points—exaggerate the swings the real economy experiences. In Wall Street parlance, people are most bullish on the eve of recessions and hysterically bearish in the early stages of recovery.[4]

The Financial Instability Hypothesis

Enter Hyman Minsky. Minsky's thesis describes a system that produces business cycle swings through the interplay of uncertainty, expectations, debt commitments, and asset prices. His key observation? As the memory of recession recedes, people become more willing to take financial risks again. This describes a population doing the opposite of what we witnessed in Never Never Land.

What happens when people increase their risk appetites as expansions age? The small disappointments that all economies deliver will turn out to have exaggerated consequences. Why? Because many businesses and individuals will have locked themselves into big debt contracts. To service these debts they need good times to continue. In other words, when a large group of individuals find themselves in Hanna's position, the overall economy suffers (see Table 4.1). And

Table 4.1
___
Minsky's Margin of Safety

- People, companies, and countries all face the same survival challenge. To avoid default they must generate enough cash, or have enough cash on hand, to meet their cash commitments.
- When cash inflows don't cover cash payments, sales of assets–stocks, bonds, factories, and homes–are necessary to forestall bankruptcy.
- Margins of safety are calibrated based on how easy it is to come up with the money to honor cash commitments.

recall, as well, that when a good many borrowers are in trouble, the lenders are in trouble too.

Minsky believed that attitudes toward risk change in stages (see Table 4.2). Early in cycles people are tentative and they *hedge* their bets. Debt use is conservative and cash cushions are plentiful. As expansions age, people become more *speculative* and debt excesses grow.

Late in expansions a growing number of people begin to act like Hanna. They enter into strategies that depend on climbing prices for their key assets. Higher asset prices provide them with the means to borrow more money to service debts that the day-to-day funds they generate simply cannot support. Minsky called this final stage *Ponzi finance.* In a true Ponzi scheme, as Bernard L. Madoff spectacularly reminded us, proceeds from new investors are used to make it appear that impressive returns are accruing to existing investors. In Hanna's case, she and her banker conned themselves into believing that servicing debts by taking on more debt was a reasonable plan. In Minsky's construct, the U.S. housing market in 2003-2007 was the mother and father of all Ponzi finance periods in U.S. history.

Both the housing bubble and the dot-com frenzy of the late 1990s show that people's attitudes about the future, at times, can become spectacularly irrational. These events are easy to analyze using Minsky's framework. But crazy notions about the future are not necessary for the financial instability hypothesis to unfold. Instead, one need only assert that, over time, conviction levels about the sustainability of a benign backdrop build. One of Minsky's great insights was his anticipation of the "Paradox of Goldilocks." Because rising conviction about a benign future, in turn, evokes rising commitment to risk, the system becomes increasingly *vulnerable* to retrenchment,

Minsky's Three Stages of Capitalist Finance

Hedge Finance:

- Early cycle, with vivid memories of recession in place.
- Conservative estimates of cash inflows are used when making financing decisions. Thus business as usual will provide more than enough money to pay cash commitments.
- Cash on hand is available, in any case, to cover disappointments.
- Debt commitments tend to be long-term fixed interest rate.
- Cash is available to pay off both the interest and principal, so refinancing is not needed.
- The margin of safety is high.

Speculative Finance:

- Mid-cycle, after several Goldilocks growth years.
- Consensus estimates of cash inflows are considered "dependable estimates." Therefore, debt levels rise. Expected cash inflows, if they arrive, provide only enough money to make interest payments on debts. Debts are "rolled over."
- Cash on hand for emergencies, shrinks.
- Debt becomes shorter term and must be continuously refinanced. This makes the borrower hostage to short-term changes in lender's willingness to extend credit.
- The margin of safety is lower.

Ponzi Finance:

- Late cycle, only distant memories of recession remain.
- Consensus estimates of cash flows ARE NOT expected to cover cash commitments.
- Cash for emergencies is all but missing.
- Debts are short term.
- Extra cash needed, in theory, will be collected by borrowing more against assets.
- Climbing asset prices, therefore, are essential for debt payments to be honored.
- The margin of safety is extremely low.

notwithstanding the fact that consensus expectations remain *reasonable* relative to recent history.

In sum, almost everyone recognizes that lunatic levels of enthusiasm invite large economic declines. Minsky's insight is that widespread comfort in the enduring nature of benign times also invites destabilizing methods of finance, which ultimately produce economic declines from small initial disappointments.

It Really Is an Uncertain World

Alpha types don't like to talk about the speculative nature of things to come. If you are in charge, you have to make decisions. Thus, even though most decisions have a boilerplate warning attached, discussions tend to focus on a small range of outcomes. The simple truth is that in order to get on with everyday business, all of us must act as if we have a sense of what lies ahead. As the cartoon guru in Figure 4.1 reminds us, however, when it comes to the future, nobody knows!

Moreover, at times, collective confidence in our vision is high and yet reality turns out to be radically different. Think back to 2001. There was widespread agreement that a multi-trillion-dollar surplus would build up over the first decade of the new millennium. Alan Greenspan was completely on board. It is instructive to revisit how confident he was about the surplus.

In late January 2001, Greenspan warned that budget surpluses were likely to be dangerously *large*.[5] He embraced calls to cut taxes in order to limit the scope of the surplus. How genuine was the surplus story in Greenspan's eyes? Greenspan was aggressive, claiming that for a wide range of possible outcomes the national debt would be paid off as the decade came to a close. As he put it:

Figure 4.1

Indeed, in almost any credible baseline scenario, short of a major and prolonged economic contraction, the full benefits of debt reduction are now achieved before the end of this decade—a prospect that did not seem likely only a year or even six months ago.[6]

Enter Ben Bernanke, in early 2006. The new U.S. Federal Reserve Board chairman also had genuine concerns about the U.S. government's budget outlook. His angst, however, reflected worries about an unending stream of deficits:

The prospective increase in the budget deficit will place at risk future living standards of our country. As a result, I think it would be very desirable to take concrete steps to lower the prospective path of the deficit.[7]

Moreover, as Chairman Bernanke explained it, dire risks loomed in the out years. By the year 2040, "absent [appropriate] actions, we would see widening and eventually unsustainable budget deficits, which would impede capital accumulation, slow economic growth, threaten financial stability, and put a heavy burden of debt on our children and grandchildren."[8]

Thus, in the span of five years, conventional wisdom, dutifully articulated by the U.S. Federal Reserve Board chairmen, completely flip-flopped on its sense of the U.S. government's budgetary situation. Worry about swelling surpluses gave way to the nightmare of accumulating deficits. In five short years! Small wonder, then, that there are more jokes about economists than any other profession save lawyers.

But the joke, of course, is on all of us. Because *everyone* charged with making economic choices is compelled to speculate about what the future will bring. In Never Never Land, rational agents have a pretty good handle on the pattern of things to come. Minsky simply reminds us that in the real world, pervasive uncertainty is the rule. The Greenspan/Bernanke about-face on the U.S. budget makes it clear that talk about the future always amounts to speculating.

Conventional Wisdom: Yesterday's News Shapes Opinion about Tomorrow

The grand miscalculation on the U.S. budget outlook makes it clear that the future can be tough to anticipate. Nonetheless, nearly everyone spends part of the day imagining an economic hereafter.

Most of us recognize that the future is unknowable. But the need to make economic choices compels us to speculate about what the future will bring.

Forced to forecast, how do people make judgments about what is on the horizon? Thirty years as a Wall Street forecaster leads me to the following simple conclusion. Most people's opinion about the future is that it will extend the trends they have witnessed in the recent past. People's opinions about the future change, for the most part, only when they are confronted with changing economic circumstances.

On a real-time basis, information about emerging trends is processed, leading to the shaping of a baseline of opinion about ongoing economic performance. Spend some time watching CNBC and the process reveals itself. The consensus outlook for the economy looks for more of the same. There are always mavericks voicing contrary opinions. But the conventional view about what comes next almost never changes in the midst of a trend.[9]

Are people acting irrationally by adopting a strategy that says tomorrow will look a lot like yesterday? Not really. Most of the time, tomorrow bears a close resemblance to yesterday. After all, both industry and economic trends tend to last for years, not for days. Once we acknowledge that we confront a world of pervasive uncertainty, it is quite reasonable to decide that, until circumstances change, we will plan as if present circumstances are likely to persist.

A majority of economic forecasters, it turns out, also rely on this rearview mirror method of forecasting. And that explains the painful fact that the economic forecasting community, as a group, failed to predict the arrival of each and every recession over the past 30 years. When economists are confronted with deteriorating economic statistics, they acknowledge that a recession is the risk, but until the downturn grips the data, they project continued economic growth.

Since the economy is not in a recession 80 percent of the time, the safe strategy is to predict recessions only when they have already arrived! That means you're right 80 percent of the time! Simply put, forecasting the recent past is the safe way to go, and it is the dominant strategy employed by professional forecasters. Indeed, no less a giant among economists than Paul Samuelson endorsed the methodology some years ago. When asked how far into the future a good economist could forecast, he replied, "One quarter back."

A String of Happy Yesterdays Builds Conviction and Invites Risky Finance

How confident will you be about your vision of the future? The longer a trend stays in place, the more people's conviction levels build. Coming out of a recession, a year's worth of reasonable growth with low inflation will likely move the conventional view toward expecting the same for the year to follow. But the consensus will also let you know that people still have great misgivings about the future. After all, less than two years back they witnessed the turmoil that attends economic decline.

What about after four or five years of good growth with low inflation? At that juncture the conventional wisdom will not have changed much, on the face of it. More of the same as an opinion about the future will lead the majority to expect another period of good growth and low inflation—just as it did after a year or so of recovery. It's likely, however, that there will now be a big change in the conviction level about the outlook. Five years of good growth, in a world where the recent past informs opinion about the future, will translate to strong confidence in the supposedly good year about to unfold.

Of course, if we parachuted in people from Never Never Land, they would be forming a different outlook. With no specific reason to expect calamity, we can conjecture that they too would venture that the best guess for next year is another year like last year. *But* Never Never Landers would be losing confidence about the enduring nature of the upturn. Recall that they have conviction about how their world works because they believe their economy is locked in a cyclical pattern. More to the point, they are cocksure about the inevitability of periodic economic decline. As a consequence, Never Never Landers will reduce exposure to risky assets, bracing for the inevitable bout of bad news that their sense of history tells them is coming.

In the real world, an extended period of calm builds confidence, and bankers, investors, entrepreneurs, and home buyers take on more risk.

Leveraged Wagers on Benign Outcomes Can Kill the Golden Goose

I emphasized earlier in this chapter that irrational exuberance on Wall Street is not necessary to derail happy times on Main Street. A Goldilocks backdrop on Main Street, over time, invites destabilizing bets on Wall Street, market mayhem, and recession for the real economy. That is the Paradox of Goldilocks that eludes conventional thinkers.

Suppose the economy registers several years of reasonably good growth with low inflation and healthy corporate profits. Let's suppose further that this backdrop delivers okay gains for stocks. As this not-too-exciting backdrop repeats itself, people gain confidence that it will endure. Some investors with a penchant for risk taking will then begin to invent ways to magnify the modest gains that stocks offer.

An investment of $100,000 will only earn you $10,000 per year. You can leverage your investment. Simply borrow $500,000 and lay that alongside your $100,000. Invest in stocks with 6-to-1 leverage and you net almost 60 percent in returns in a world of 10 percent stock market gains. To restate the key point, you are not betting that the world will turn out much better than okay—so you don't have irrational expectations about the future. But you have made a very big bet that okay arrives. If it doesn't, things go awry, big-time.

Clearly, conservative investors can ignore a 10 percent pullback, happy in their commitment to the long term. A 6-to-1 leveraged speculator, in contrast, faces a grim reality. The $600,000 invested falls by $60,000. But the speculator owes $500,000 and some interest. Her underlying cash falls to a bit less than $40,000, an outsized loss considering the modest disappointment that arrived from Main Street.

What happens to the markets and the economy if a great many investors made leveraged wagers? Initially, stock market gains exceed the economy's performance as big borrowing provides cash to bid up share prices. A big jump for share prices will stimulate both company investing and consumer spending. Suddenly, a Goldilocks economy will begin to heat up. The consequent rise for profits will justify the climb for share prices. But the boom facilitated by leveraged finance will put pressure on wages and prices. When monetary authorities tighten credit in response to somewhat higher inflation, the economy will slow.

At this point, however, the leap for stocks in place requires strong profit gains to support prices. In these inflated circumstances, a modest slowing is very disappointing to owners of stock. Moreover, because of the leveraged nature of their wagers, they lose substantial wealth and become rapid sellers. The real economy is then hit with falling share prices, falling investment, and falling consumer spending. In short, a recession is taking hold. Importantly, the dynamic that produced the downturn was not crazy enthusiasm about the future. All that was required was aggressive wagers on a continuation of a Goldilocks backdrop. This is the Paradox of Goldilocks.

History Confirms It: Risky Finance Flourishes as the Good Times Roll

Increasing use of risky finance, the past 25 years makes clear, squares with the world investors live in. Consider the chart in Figure 4.2. It represents investor willingness to lend to risky companies over the

Figure 4.2

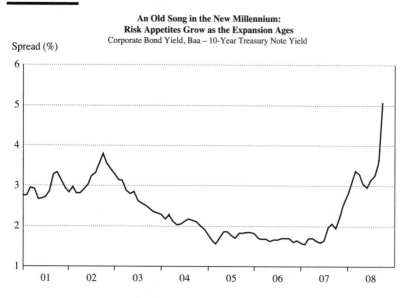

An Old Song in the New Millennium:
Risk Appetites Grow as the Expansion Ages
Corporate Bond Yield, Baa – 10-Year Treasury Note Yield

Spread (%)

first eight years of the twenty-first century. Not surprisingly, we see that corporations found that funds were very expensive in 2001-2002 amidst the recession. Bankruptcies are common during recessions. As the expansion aged, however, confidence built. And with that confidence we see shrinking borrowing costs over each of the first seven years. Never Never Landers might have begun to worry about an imminent recession as the economy logged several years of good gains. But real-world investors increased their enthusiasm for risky bonds as the expansion grew long in the tooth.

A one-cycle phenomenon? In the 1990s, risk taking was most visible in the stock market. Price/earnings ratios—comparing the price of stocks to the companies' underlying earnings—soared into early 2000. Thus, as Figure 4.3 shows, people were buying shares at ever higher prices, relative to the companies' economic performances, throughout

Figure 4.3

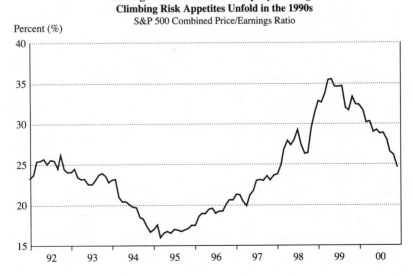

**Soaring Stocks Relative to Company Earnings:
Climbing Risk Appetites Unfold in the 1990s**
S&P 500 Combined Price/Earnings Ratio

Figure 4.4

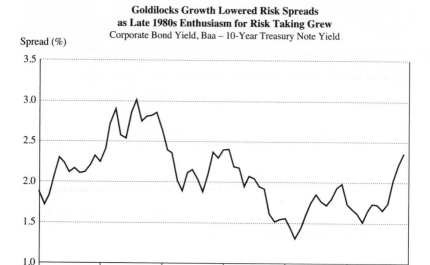

**Goldilocks Growth Lowered Risk Spreads
as Late 1980s Enthusiasm for Risk Taking Grew**
Corporate Bond Yield, Baa – 10-Year Treasury Note Yield

the 1990s expansion. And in the 1980s? Figure 4.4 shows that risky corporate bond rates fell irregularly versus Treasury borrowing costs for most of the second half of the decade.

Taken together, the charts in Figures 4.2, 4.3, and 4.4 make it quite clear that risk appetites grow as expansions age, just as the analysis suggests they will.

Margins of Safety and Company Leverage

As can be seen in the charts, shrinking borrowing costs for risky companies are the rule as an economy grows. Not surprisingly, companies are likely to borrow a lot more money if rates are low. Company CEOs and CFOs, after several years of good growth, are also likely to have inflated confidence about their business prospects in the years to come. Combine confidence in future sales with easy credit terms, and businesses begin to borrow aggressively.

Remember, Hanna figured out that by borrowing twice as much as Hal, she could leave him in the dust, despite the same initial cash. So too with businesses. Companies increase their debts, relative to their sales levels, as expansions age. Wall Street celebrates this increased leverage, at least for most of the economic cycle.

Nonetheless, as company debt payments climb relative to sales and profits, they become increasingly sensitive to a bout of disappointing business. Simply put, businesses shrink their margins of safety as economic growth continues. That puts them in compromised positions when the inevitable disappointment arises.

Conclusion: Increasing Risk Comes Naturally, and Leads to Boom and Bust Cycles

In the early stages of most recessions a common lament is uttered:

Who could have foreseen . . .

In 1990, Saddam Hussein invaded Kuwait. Clearly, mainstream forecasters are ill equipped to predict a madman's suicidal military misadventure. Nonetheless, economic developments in the United States from late 1989 through 1992 had very little to do with the Mideast and oil prices. The war was the catalyst for the recession; the debt excesses were the driver.

In 2000, the initial fall for technology shares was blamed on rising inflation and Fed tightening. The devastation of 9/11 explained subsequent retrenchment. But in the fullness of time we learned that the brave-new-world boom of the 1990s was more about financial system excess than about productivity-enhancing technologies.

In 2007, house prices began to fall. No big surprise there. But when the declines became large, conventional analysts covered their tracks. "Who could have foreseen such breathtaking falls?" As we learned from Hanna's financing strategy, a small fall all but ensured a large fall. Thus, what did you need to precipitate a big recession in 2008? A small fall was all!

In summation, risky finance exaggerates the consequences of small disappointments. When trying to understand the unrelenting nature of boom and bust cycles in a capitalist economy, look no further than finance.

Chapter | 5

FREE MARKET CAPITALISM: STILL THE SUPERIOR STRATEGY

To Get Rich Is Glorious
—China's official slogan during Deng Xiaoping's early reforms

If we agree that the financial markets drive the boom and bust cycle, should we also embrace the notion that the stock and bond markets are solely a source of economic instability? Not at all. Capitalist finance, in nonstop pursuit of profits, has allocated economic resources in an impressive fashion over the past 50 years. The near-complete elimination of command-based strategies for economic organization in China and the former Soviet states was an unmistakable victory for the Free World on the issue of markets versus planning. Markets, on both Main Street and Wall Street, are simply much better at allocating resources and delivering economic growth. We can look at the period from the 1950s through the 1990s as one long economic experiment. The data are in; the market strategy has emphatically triumphed.

Moreover, great economic thinkers have long linked the predisposition to boom with the persistence of impressive economic growth. The Austrian economist Joseph Schumpeter celebrated the dynamism of entrepreneurs—individuals who he thought possessed the skills needed to master technological advances. Their activities, he asserted, drive productivity higher to the ultimate benefit of the national citizenry. From Schumpeter's perspective, periods of economic retrenchment are inevitable. Hyman Minsky simply expanded upon Schumpeter's ideas; no doubt it helped that Schumpeter was one of Minsky's dissertation advisors at Harvard. For Minsky, periodic financial market upheaval—the Wall Street analogue to Schumpeter's creative destruction on Main Street—is equally unavoidable.

Both great minds, therefore, saw recurring retrenchment as inevitable in a free market economy. But Minsky distinguished between the cleansing nature of failure and bankruptcies on Main Street and the potentially disastrous consequences of panics and modern day bank runs on Wall Street—correctly, I believe. The history of the past 50 years validates the essential teachings of both Schumpeter and Minsky. Entrepreneurs, bankrolled by investment managers, do lift living standards, just as Schumpeter said they did. But enlightened capitalists also need to acknowledge that a free hand at the central bank—and occasionally a large-sized government bailout—are absolutely necessary. They turn out to be the antidote to the financial system excesses that Minsky correctly points out arrive as every cycle comes to an end.

The simple truth is that Schumpeter and his student, Hyman Minsky, deserve coequal status when thinking about modern day capitalism as we go forward. Free market ideologues can protest about government intervention. And free market naysayers can deny the fruits of the efforts of entrepreneurs and investors. But history has the final word. And the history of the postwar years leads me to the following conclusion about free market systems:

> Capitalism is best at delivering the goods. Creative destruction on Main Street is simply the price of progress. Simultaneously, destabilizing market upheavals come with the territory in free market societies. Thus, government rescue operations are an inescapable cost of capitalism.

Why Socializing Investment Is a Bad Idea

Just as creative destruction is a bad idea for banks, socialized investment is a bad idea in general. The genius of Wall Street finance is not about its superior analytic capabilities relative to Washington policy elites. It is instead about the power of failure to keep capital moving to intelligent places.

I began my career as a student of government investments, not of stocks and bonds. My dissertation investigated the usefulness of cost/benefit analysis as a substitute for revenue and cost projections made by budding companies. What I discovered was straightforward. When companies projected revenues and spent money, they were often too optimistic about their revenue inflows. And they pulled out or went bankrupt. But government projects, once they began to spend money, faced no such discipline. Benefits, as it turns out, are in the eyes of the bureaucrat. They can be redefined again and again so as to perpetually justify investment projects. Indeed, at the worst, we can find ourselves authorizing *bridges to nowhere*!

Clearly, as I detailed in the previous chapter, the spectacular rescue efforts put in place in the autumn of 2008 were an absolutely necessary effort to protect the safety and soundness of the financial system. But these rescue efforts are not good policy for the economy in general. Countless bankruptcies go on in a capitalist economy—bankruptcies that ensure that bad ideas fall by the wayside. Innovation is the process of making the existing order obsolete. For new ideas to flourish, the old way has to wither away. Figure 5.1 makes it clear that bankruptcy filings are a permanent fixture in the United States.

As emphasized previously, creative destruction—and the bankruptcies that are its hallmark—is the price of progress.

In a world in which government controls investment, bad ideas get perpetual funding. To state the obvious, socialized investment, the strategy of the former Soviet Bloc, was an unambiguous failure. Innovation was squashed. The cleansing powers of creative destruction were absent. This led to a stepwise deterioration in efficiency and a buildup in waste.

Figure 5.1

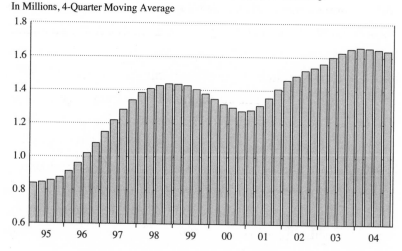

**Bankruptcy Filings: Most of the Time,
They Are the Price of Progress**
U.S. Bankruptcy Courts: Total Bankruptcy Petition Filings
In Millions, 4-Quarter Moving Average

Late in the process, countries in the Soviet Bloc were completely out of touch with the desires of their citizenries. Simply put, though we can't let the banking system experience creative destruction, we must celebrate the free market's ability to rapidly direct investment dollars. Most of the time it is a breathtakingly efficient and dynamic operation.

Globalization: A Capital Markets Phenomenon

Over the past 20 years, capital markets have been the main force driving the globalization of the world's economy. Those against globalization can point to the 2008-2009 global recession as a powerful example of what can go wrong. Nonetheless, the economic facts of global life that have accumulated on the ground over the past 25 years cannot be ignored. Nearly 1 billion people in Asia escaped abject poverty as free-flowing capital financed development on a scale that dwarfed anything the World Bank or aid agencies could have imagined a few decades ago.

China is the poster child for the benefits of globalization. Nearly half a billion Chinese citizens joined the twenty-first century after living in near feudal circumstances during the reign of Mao. Think about infant mortality rates in the many poverty-ridden countries of Africa: China's economic circumstances were comparable when reforms began in 1979. The 400 million Chinese who escaped abject poverty left behind a world of rampant death and disease. The country's willingness to link its economy to global trade and capital flows, of course, means that its economy now sags when recession grips the developed world. But the unprecedented progress of the past 25 years should be sufficient evidence for the Chinese that the boom and bust cycle is worth the ride.

The fantastic transformation in China after the death of Mao required a new paradigm. One China scholar, writing in the late 1980s, captured the newfound capitalist instincts:

> During those free-for-all months of 1986, perhaps the most implausible headline about economics I saw was "Bankruptcy Improves Businesses." The August New China News Agency dispatch told how . . . an experimental bankruptcy law . . . would "eliminate backward companies through competition," a phenomenon that, in spite of socialist China's commitment to the working class, [was] referred to as "progressive."[1]

Schumpeter no doubt would have smiled ear-to-ear had he lived to see his insights take hold in a former communist giant.

The World of Finance: Nonstop Reassessment

In a modern capitalist economy, economic agents in all sectors are compelled to make both brick-and-mortar and lending and borrowing decisions. As households, corporations, governments, and central banks make investment and financing decisions, the sum of their transactions are visible in real time on computer terminals.

The entire constellation of asset prices—stocks, bonds, currencies, commodities, futures, options—adjusts as opinions about economic prospects change. Indeed, if one embraces the efficient market hypothesis, the price of a capital asset is the embodiment of the present value of incomes to be received in the future. Thus, every decision to buy or sell implies a judgment of what the future will be like. One can look at a blinking Bloomberg screen as a streaming, nonstop reassessment of the consensus forecast. Investors vote with dollars.

And—so long as wealth is not too concentrated—the majority, not the chosen few, carries the day.

Moment by moment, emerging information shapes a baseline of opinion about ongoing economic performance. The consensus outlook, by processing news in lightning fashion, updates the snapshot of the recent past—and expectations for the future change if and when the emerging reality changes. The consensus opinion about the outlook for overall trends and the implied forecasts embedded in financial market asset prices are the products of the interplay of all actors in the system. Corporate CEOs, government policy makers, Wall Street analysts and economists, TV commentators, consumers, and print journalists all collaborate in its creation, care, and feeding (see Figure 5.2).

Thus, the real-time changes in asset prices, interest rates, currencies, and the like provide an up-to-the-second consensus opinion to the trained eye about what the future will bring. In the movie *The Matrix*, Neo learns to see past the code streaming across the green screen and visualize the world it implies. Professional economists, analysts, strategists, money managers, and hedge fund speculators

Figure 5.2

The Real World/Financial Market Processing of Information

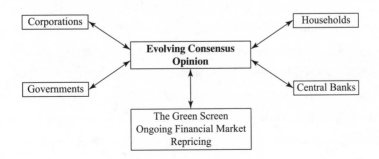

essentially do the same thing. As they contemplate their Bloomberg screens, they see how opinions about the world ahead are evolving.

Emerging company, industry, and sector developments inform opinion about the economic entities in question and also influence attitudes about overall economic prospects. Likewise, changing sentiments about aggregate trajectories at times weigh on opinion about company, industry, and sector prospects. In Wall Street jargon, bottom-up and top-down opinion influence one another.

Obviously, company projections, macroeconomic forecasts, and TV talking head commentary are different animals. Companies care about sales rates and bottom lines. Economywide forecasts attempt to present a consistent vision of the future for major economic barometers. News coverage must be instantaneous and entertaining. Nonetheless, most conjecture about the future shares a common language and arithmetic. Talk almost always compares emerging news to previous expectations. Growth rates, not levels, are in focus. Moreover, we are most captivated by evidence of changes in growth rates, not in the ascent to new levels nor in the extension of ongoing trends. As my dad, a physicist, liked to put it, "It's a second derivative world."

Capitalist Finance Drives Schumpeter's Innovation Machine

This immediate processing of news, to constantly reshape our vision of the future, provides spectacular benefits to capitalist economies. As the news shapes opinion, it rewards success and punishes failure. In particular, money pours into areas where innovative approaches revolutionize effort. Wall Street, on a real-time basis, shines a spotlight on such successes. And success, for a long while, breeds imitation and more success. In that fashion, capital markets channel funds toward innovative and therefore lucrative endeavors, and deny funds to anti-quated enterprises. Real-time, 24/7, Wall Street feeds the innovation machine. For Schumpeter, this is God's work:

> [In] capitalist reality as distinguished from its textbook picture, it is not [price] competition which counts but the competition from the new commodity, the new technology, the new source of supply . . . which commands a decisive cost or quality advantage and which strikes not at the margins of the profits and the outputs of the existing firms but at their foundations and their very lives. [An analysis that] . . . neglects this essential element of the case . . . even if correct in logic as well as in fact, is like Hamlet without the Danish prince.[2]

Thus, capitalist finance, most of the time, provides the monetary reward system that propels Schumpeterian magic. Schumpeter's great insight was his rejection of models that looked at the world as static. His notion of creative destruction—innovations that bankrupt champions of an earlier order—transcended theories concluding that markets came to stable resting places—*equilibriums*. Thus, Schumpeter and his student, Hyman Minsky, were in complete accord when it came to the issue of the unstable nature of capitalism. For Minsky, however, upward instability over time morphs into destabilizing downturns. And that morphology takes place in the world of finance.

Conventional Thinkers Forecast the Recent Past

Capital flows engineered the great global boom of the 1985-2007 years. And the gains that arrived cannot be minimized. Nonetheless, seasoned students of financial markets know that there is a pitfall in this process. The temptation is to embrace, unequivocally, the notion of efficient markets. Over the Greenspan/Bernanke era, that was the strategy employed. Both Fed chairmen, in doing so, were able to point out that financial markets offer up the best guess that money can buy about future economic outcomes. But that strategy, history shows, guarantees that policy makers, alongside market participants, will be dumbfounded at each and every turning point. Certainly, conventional thinkers in 2007 were completely blindsided by the events culminating in the 2008 crisis.

History reveals that market participants try but generally don't anticipate change—however much they infallibly react to it. And that, straightforwardly, reflects the fact that the emerging opinion about the future is not created from powerful forecasting models. We simply don't have models that forecast history before it happens. As I noted earlier, opinions about the future change as the world collectively *discovers* real-time changes in the news flow about the recent past.

This is not meant to be an indictment of capitalist finance. To repeat, free markets create spectacularly efficient feedback mechanisms that reward success and failure. But 30 years on Wall Street suggest to me that this feedback process is largely backward looking.

U.S. Recession in 2008: Capitulation After-the-Fact

Claiming that there is a strong tendency for the conventional wisdom to extrapolate may sound unduly harsh. But imagining how the world may change requires a great deal of heavy lifting. It is really hard! And it is fraught with risk. Consider the consensus view on the U.S. economy that evolved over the course of 2008. The pattern confirms that most people believe circumstances will change only when changing circumstances are upon them.

Certainly a forecaster willing to predict that changes were afoot had plenty to go on at the start of 2008 (see Figures 5.3 and 5.4). I was quite sure the United States had entered into recession. As I wrote in January 2008:

> Over the past six months, key barometers of financial market conditions have been signaling that U.S. recession was a growing risk. More recently, as a wide variety of real economy indicators registered violent moves lower, financial system angst built to a crescendo. If we look back over the past 40 years, there are cases in which financial market recession signals turned out to be wrong. But when financial market warnings of recession are followed by real economy retrenchment, recession unfolded in every case over the past 40 years. Our guess, at present, is that the recession began in the fourth quarter of last year.[3]

My point was straightforward. Sharp falls for stock markets and violent widening for credit spreads sometimes give a false signal of recession. That happened in both 1987 and in 1998. But when violence in financial markets is followed by significant deterioration in key real economy barometers, *recession has always arrived*. Falling U.S. payrolls, declining real income, and sliding industrial production were all a reality in January 2008. Thus, it seemed to me that recession had already begun.

Figure 5.3

Recession Would Be Avoided, Consensus Asserted, through Mid-2008 Despite Plunging Share Prices...
Dow Jones Industrial Average Stock Price Index

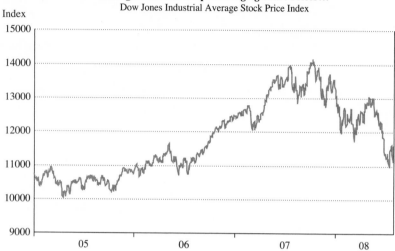

Figure 5.4

...and an Uninterrupted String of Job Losses That Came into Full View in January of 2008
Nonfarm Payroll Employment

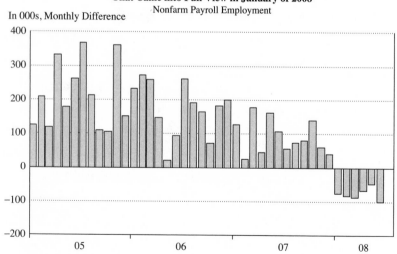

Nonetheless, consensus expectations embraced a no-recession forecast until an unambiguous swoon took hold in autumn of 2008. The Federal Reserve Board, in July 2008, put it this way:

> The economy is expected to expand slowly over the rest of this year. FOMC participants anticipate a gradual strengthening of economic growth over coming quarters as the lagged effects of past monetary policy actions, amid gradually improving financial market conditions, begin to provide additional lift to spending and as housing activity begins to stabilize.

Consensus economic forecasters did no better. As Table 5.1 reveals, continued expansion was given better than 2-to-1 odds through May of 2008. Incredibly, as late as August of 2008, forecasters believed that the fourth quarter of 2008 was more likely to expand than it was to decline. Recession was accepted as the prevailing reality in November of 2008, on the heels of widespread evidence of economic retreat. At that time the NBER, the official arbiter, also declared that the United States was in recession. It set the start date in December of

Table 5.1

Consensus Expectations:
A Forecast or an Aftcast?

Probability That GDP Would Decline*

Survey Date:	Feb 2008	May 2008	Aug 2008	Nov 2008
Quarter:				
Q3:2008	30%	29%	34%	NA
Q4:2008	23%	30%	47%	90%

*Average Expectation: Federal Reserve Bank of Philadelphia, Survey of Professional Economists

2007. Thus consensus forecasters declared the United States to be in a downturn roughly one year after it had begun.

Obviously, everyone doesn't regurgitate a simple description of the past as a best guess about the future. Indeed, I have spent the past 30 years speculating about how things could change in important ways. And I've worked with risk-taking institutional investors who have made a practice of trying to anticipate, rather than react to, change. But it is a daunting enough task to master the lessons of yesterday. The painful truth is that it takes a lot of hard work to understand the recent past. If you want to conjecture about how things might change, the possibilities abound. The conventional wisdom, not surprisingly, only changes its opinion about the future when the recent past forces the change. Major changes in economic circumstances, therefore, are destined to catch the consensus by surprise.

From Extrapolation to Excess and Upheaval

There is a second problem with extrapolating markets. Success will ultimately breed excess. We applaud the markets' ability to reward success and punish failure. Over time, however, that pushes us toward a situation in which we all begin to agree. As people become like-minded and form a herd, bubble conditions emerge, and the market steers the economy toward dangerous territory. The problem with a bubble, as we brutally witnessed twice in the first decade of this century, is that it puts everyone's eggs in the same basket. When the news flow reveals a future at odds with the conventional wisdom, the market punishes that bubble-inflated sector—and since the majority has been financing the bubble sector, its demise takes the whole economy down.

Thus, extrapolating markets predispose the economy to excessive uses of risk and concentration of investment. And the interplay of these two flaws explains each of the major economic declines of the past 25 years.

In summation, the savvy analyst must be of two minds about both efficient markets and consensus expectations. Day-to-day we can embrace adjustments in financial market asset prices and up-to-the-minute forecast revisions as efficient. And the sweep of history tells us that capitalist finance rewards the innovator and starves yesterday's approach of future funding. But over the course of a business cycle, economic history also reveals that false confidences will grow, expectations will become excessive, and the stage will be set for a bust that will test the fabric of the financial system.

How to dance between a celebration of market efficiencies and a preparation for market upheavals is the art part of intelligent policy making in a capitalist economy. How a savvy central banker might do that is the subject of the next chapter.

Chapter | 6

MONETARY POLICY: NOT THE WRONG MEN, THE WRONG MODEL

The ideas of economists and political philosophers, both when they are right and when they are wrong, are more powerful than is commonly understood. Indeed the world is ruled by little else.
—John Maynard Keynes, *The General Theory of Employment, Interest, and Money*, 1936

Amid the wreckage of the burst U.S. housing bubble, with the first serious recession since the early 1980s taking hold in 2008, it became fashionable to vilify Alan Greenspan. He was, after all, the man in charge during both the collapse of Nasdaq and the meltdown in mortgage finance. These back-to-back financial market upheavals were accompanied by recessions. But the 2008 downturn was brutal for American families, and in 2009 it is reverberating around the globe. The newly emerging story line? Alan Greenspan, throughout his tenure, was asleep at the switch.[1]

The change of opinion emerging in 2008 about the former chairman was nothing short of spectacular. Only a few years back Alan

Greenspan had been canonized. He was on the cover of *BusinessWeek* in July 1997, and Senator John McCain, in his first run at the U.S. presidency, made light of Greenspan's godlike status early in his campaign. When asked about his willingness to reappoint the chairman to a third term, McCain quipped, "If he's alive or dead, it doesn't matter. If he's dead, just prop him up and put some dark glasses on him like *Weekend at Bernie's*."

I had occasion to witness the growing Greenspan idolatry first-hand in the spring of 2000. President Bill Clinton, in April of that year, hosted the White House Conference on the New Economy, assembling 100 or so economists, Wall Street analysts, and technology company gurus for an all-day session in the West Wing. Most of the participants, including me, were surprised and impressed that the president spent a good part of the day actively involved. Bill Gates gave a lively and provocative talk. But what was truly amazing was the reverential treatment that Chairman Greenspan received when he spoke in the early afternoon. When Greenspan highlighted technology analysts' profit forecasts as the reason to expect many more years of boom, the assembled experts nearly sighed. Clinton was the president, Bill Gates was the billionaire. But Alan Greenspan was clearly the rock star at the end of the millennium all-day shindig at the White House.

Within six months Bob Woodward completed the coronation. *Maestro: Greenspan's Fed and the American Boom* hit the bookstores in November 2000 and was immediately a bestseller. The book, pure and simple, declared that Greenspan was a genius.

In *Greenspan's Bubbles*, by William Fleckenstein, published in 2008, everything is reversed. Greenspan is portrayed in this crucifixion as a combination of ignorant, arrogant, naive, and, at times, lazy.

Clearly there is no mystery to the change in assessment about Greenspan. In 2000, when Woodward wrote his book, the economy was in the tenth year of expansion, a postwar record, and stock prices had registered a record rise. In 2008, the economy was in its second recession in seven years, the collapse for house prices was unprecedented, and the stock market swoon at its lows put market averages back to levels seen in late-1996. Thus, no money had been made in stocks for over 12 years. In sum, the results were brutal, and the consequent effects on the chairman's reputation were quite predictable. Greenspan the god became Greenspan the goat.

The Wrong Man? No, the Wrong Focus

Did the Greenspan-led Fed make major errors? Absolutely. But the mistakes committed first by Alan Greenspan and afterward by Ben Bernanke were sweeping strategic errors, not minor tactical gaffs. Moreover, the Fed's strategy was crafted using beliefs that were the centerpiece of mainstream economic thinking. Thus, Greenspan and his followers used bad strategies, but the strategies reflected mainstream views. As we detail in Chapter 13, mainstream economic theory gave license to Fed policy errors over the past two decades. So ivory tower economists share a part of the blame for the mess that arrived in the world's financial markets in 2008.

Simply put, Fed policy makers consistently made three major errors over the past 25 years. They defined excesses narrowly, focusing on wages and prices. They celebrated the wisdom of market judgments. And they overestimated their power to unilaterally steer the U.S. economy in an increasingly integrated world. These strategic errors, over time, allowed excesses to accumulate. The 2008 recession and the violent retrenchment in the world of finance can be laid at the doorstep of these three grand miscalculations.

Nonetheless, it is a big mistake to lay the blame for these errors solely on Alan Greenspan. To be sure, he was a cheerleader for the boom that defined most of the past 25 years. But there is no denying that his strategy was the product of a vision embraced by mainstream thinkers throughout his tenure at the Fed. How else can we explain the fact that the world at large celebrated his actions and hung on his every word? He was labeled "the Maestro" precisely because the world perceived him to be perfectly in tune with the global economy's needs. The problem, therefore, lay in the macroeconomic foundations that gave rise to Greenspan-accommodated excesses.

Taking Away the Punch Bowl, a Long-Standing Tradition

Since the end of the Second World War, U.S. central bankers have known what their job was all about. William McChesney Martin, who ran the Federal Reserve Board from 1951 to 1970, put it this way: "Our job is to take away the punch bowl, just when the party is getting good." In other words, Fed policy makers are supposed to be in charge of reining in economywide excesses. They have the power to increase or lower the economy's growth rate by tightening or easing credit conditions.[2] Obviously, most of the world wants as much growth as possible. Fed policy makers, therefore, try to deliver as much growth as they can without producing excesses that will derail growth sometime down the road.

Why not keep interest rates super low and flood the economy with money, letting it grow as fast as it possibly can? Without getting bogged down in theory, we can simply say that if the Fed floods the system with money, excesses develop. These excesses seem pleasant at first. Over time, however, an overheating economy will crash and burn.

Let me share my own experience with dangerous spurts in order to make the point that long-run sustainable speeds are the right target.

When I was in my 30s, I ran the Honolulu marathon for three years in a row. The second time, I ran the race in three hours and 30 minutes, my best time. On average, I ran at an eight minute per mile pace. Because the marathon began at 6 A.M., when it was cool, I used to run the first two miles at a much faster pace — something like six minutes per mile. The third time I ran the race, however, I had a most unusual experience. And I took away from that experience a life lesson.

As was my norm, I began the race in high gear. Very early on in the race, however, a fellow runner began to talk to me about the event while we were running. She was a serious marathoner, new to this race and looking for local knowledge. She spoke. I answered. She queried again. I answered. She began to get quite chatty. I responded when a question was asked. This went on for about 20 minutes. And then I realized that I was well into my third mile at a six minute per mile pace. Suddenly I had a brainstorm. Maybe I had been denying myself much better marathon times simply because I didn't have the courage to run faster. Maybe 26 miles at six minutes per mile was doable. And so, with the hope that a great time was on the near-term horizon, and in part to avoid the embarrassment of slowing down sharply in front of my newfound friend, I decided that this marathon — for as long as it could be — would be for me a six mile per minute affair.

And so it was for more than 12 miles. For the first half dozen, in fact, it was wildly exhilarating. Running fast, with the elite runners, listening to the chatty gazelle next to me, and feeling no major stresses,

I became nearly euphoric. But then, slowly at first, and unmistakably thereafter, the pains began. My legs became heavy, and my sides began to cramp. Even my arms were cramping up. When we hit the mid-mark, 13.1 miles, my soon-to-disappear friend let out with a cheery cry. "Halfway home, and we're set to break three hours!" At that point I succumbed to reality.

"Not me, dear," I said, embarrassed. "I think four hours are in the cards for this cowboy today." I stopped dead in my tracks and saw the gazelle stare back at me with a queer look on her face as she flew away. I ended up walking for three miles, until the cramps subsided. My final time? An embarrassing four hours and 16 minutes.

But the lesson was learned. Don't be seduced by the notion that your fastest sprint can be sustained. Your best time, over the long haul, will be achieved if you pace yourself.

Denying Irrational Exuberance and Embracing a Brave New World

Alan Greenspan, metaphorically, met up with his own gazelle in 1997. In December 1996, with the U.S. stock market soaring, he gave a speech declaring that share prices were rising too rapidly. He warned that U.S. equity markets were in the grip of irrational exuberance.

In response, for a few days the stock market retreated. But over the next six months, the U.S. economy grew rapidly, inflation stayed low, and share prices continued their rapid ascent. A growing chorus of mainstream economic thinkers pointed to tame inflation as confirmation that this surprisingly fast growth rate was not producing excesses.

In June 1997, Greenspan embraced the building consensus and made it the new conventional wisdom. The U.S. economy had a new higher speed limit. We had entered a "brave new world," thanks to technology gains from computers. Stock prices were not exuberant, they were prescient. The soaring stock market, the consensus declared, had simply figured out what analysts came to understand soon afterward. An unprecedented boom, with minimal inflation, was on the horizon.

For three years the U.S. economy did boom. Quite incredibly, inflation fell during the boom, even as the U.S. unemployment rate fell to levels not seen since the middle 1960s. A boom without excesses is every economist's definition of nirvana. It really did seem that we were in a brave new world.

But the boom, as we all know, eventually came crashing down. Nasdaq fell by nearly 80 percent. Technology investment imploded. Brave-new-world assertions gave way to fears of deep recession. Greenspan was forced to collapse overnight interest rates to insulate the full economy from the swoon unfolding in technology. In 2002, for a short while, a growing chorus began to question the policy of benign neglect toward asset markets. But the doubts soon disappeared.

Why was the lesson of the 1990s asset boom and bust cycle lost on mainstream thinkers? Unquestionably, the strikingly mild nature of the 2001 U.S. recession seemed to validate at least a fair amount of the conventional wisdom. If the mildest recession on record was the only price we had to pay for the record length expansion of the 1990s, then Greenspan and mainstream thinkers had been mostly right. It had not turned out to be a perpetual boom, but it did preserve the long expansion/mild recession pattern begun in the last cycle. The lesson seemed simple: keep inflation low, ignore the financial markets unless they need rescue, and bask in the glory of the Great Moderation.

A Model Aimed at Stabilizing Our Economic Future

Times change. Ben Bernanke, Greenspan's successor, declared in October 2008 that asset markets needed to be added to the Fed's list of potentially destabilizing excesses. Why? Sadly, it was not the force of ideas that carried the day. It was the end of the Great Moderation. The breathtaking nature of the financial crisis and the depth and breadth of real economy retrenchment put an end to the notion that policy makers had the magic formula. Bernanke's concession about Wall Street's role in the 2008 upheaval was simply a statement of the obvious.

But to genuinely change attitudes about the right way to steer the United States and other economies around the world, the essential way we think about our economy needs to change. The two previous chapters of this book make the case that financial markets can be a major source of instability for the real economy. This self-evident truth needs to be incorporated into mainstream thinking. Only then will policy makers have the right footing for a reshaping of monetary policy.

I have no doubt that a majority of mainstream thinkers will fight this change, notwithstanding the carnage that befell the global economy in 2008. As I detail in Chapter 13, making financial market upheaval the driver of economic cycles creates theoretical problems for most academic economists of both red state and blue state persuasion. But the history of economic thought makes it clear that new formulations take hold amidst economic circumstances that destroy the conventional wisdom. This, quite simply, is just such a moment.

How will defenders of the status quo explain the crisis of 2008? Economic downturns, according to mainstream theory, result from either a destabilizing rise in inflation or an unanticipated shock to the economic system. Conveniently, mainstream thinkers were indeed shocked by the events of 2008. Shock in hand, they can argue that their sense of the way the world works is intact. Listen to speeches from representatives of the European Central Bank, the ECB, and all appears to be right as rain. A summary version of their postcrisis commentary goes something like this:

> The 2008 crisis was a onetime financial market shock. It changed the outlook for economic activity and inflation. We are responding accordingly. Come tomorrow, however, we will refocus on wages and prices. We offer this assessment secure in the belief that we are successfully conducting policy. For as bad as the shock of 2008 was, it was fundamentally unpredictable. It was, quite simply, a bolt from the blue.

But enlightened spectators of the economic scene should now know that is sheer nonsense. The asset excesses that sloshed around the globe as we approached 2008 were there for all to see. As they were in Japan in the 1980s and the United States in the 1990s and the 1920s. Monetary policy makers must end their policy of benign neglect toward asset markets.

Clearly, the paradox that confounded mainstream thinking in the decades that led up to the 2008 crisis is that Goldilocks growth on Main Street invites destabilizing activities on Wall Street. Hy Minsky understood this decades before the phrase "Goldilocks economy" had been coined. Enlightened capitalists should insist that mainstream economists and policy makers incorporate his vision into their thinking. In so doing, they will help us form a strategy for stabilizing global economies in the years ahead.

Part | **II**

ECONOMIC EXPERIENCE: 1985-2002

Chapter | 7

HOW FINANCIAL INSTABILITY EMERGED IN THE 1980s

In economies where borrowing and lending exist, ingenuity
goes into developing and introducing financial innovations,
just as into production and marketing innovations.
—Hyman Minsky, *John Maynard Keynes*, 2008

In the middle 1980s it became clear that the two-decade battle with the Great Inflation had been won. The brutal back-to-back recessions, 1980-1982, had cut inflation to low single digits. In 1986, when oil prices collapsed, the celebration became raucous. Confidence in low inflation gave rise to belief in a long expansion.

With conviction about blue skies ahead, financial engineers began to work their magic. In the stock market, large mutual funds and other institutional investors were presented with a new invention aimed at locking in their gains and still allowing them to stay invested. In the banking world, Savings & Loans were offered a new product that would allow them to become bankers to mid-sized companies without creating large loan offices. Both innovations, on the face of it, seemed too good to be true. And in fact both of them were.

Portfolio Insurance and the 1987 Crash

The unambiguous victory against inflation was great for stock and bond prices. The big move down for price pressures ushered in a sharp fall for interest rates.[1] Falling interest rates, in turn, raised the value of future company earnings, and share prices soared.[2] The great gains in stock prices, 1982-1986, were a welcome change. Seasoned money managers remembered all too well the brutal 1970s, with the Dow no higher in the summer of 1982 than in the fall of 1971. This presented a quandary. Low inflation was a reason to be optimistic about the prospects for both the economy and the stock market. But the gains achieved in the mid-1980s were so large that professional managers were desperate for a way to lock them into place.

Wall Street wizards came to the rescue. Portfolio insurance was invented. The concept was simple. Money managers could keep their portfolios invested in stocks, but to protect their gains, they bought stock options that locked in their automatic sell orders if the market were to fall back to a specified level.

Think of it like this: I own a stock at $120. I am up 20 percent, but I don't want to sell, since I see good times ahead. That said, I also want to make sure that I keep at least a 10 percent gain, even if the market begins to sink. So I arrange with a Wall Street firm, ahead of time, to sell the stock if it ever goes below $110. Hey, I can have my cake and eat it too!

The problem arrived with a vengeance in the fall of 1987. It turns out that a great many money managers had locked in automatic sell orders. And most of the sell orders were triggered at around the same price level for the overall market. When the economy surprised on the upside in 1987 and inflation began to rise, the U.S. Federal Reserve Board began raising interest rates. The climb for interest rates scared some investors into selling. And in October 1987, in a wild display of ingenuity gone haywire, thousands of institutional investors watched their automatic sell orders kick in on the same day, flooding the market with unwanted stock and delivering a one day 25 percent decline for the Dow (see Figure 7.1).

In the immediate aftermath of the crash, widespread panic about another Great Depression gripped the world. The U.S. Federal Reserve Board temporarily collapsed overnight interest rates to provide liquidity to the system. A few weeks later it officially lowered its target for overnight rates, fearing Main Street repercussions from the Wall Street meltdown.

Figure 7.1

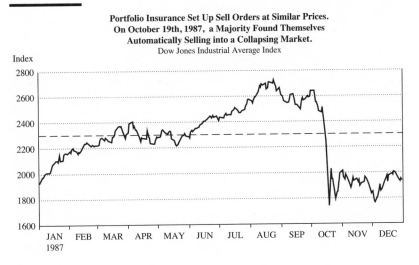

Portfolio Insurance Set Up Sell Orders at Similar Prices.
On October 19th, 1987, a Majority Found Themselves
Automatically Selling into a Collapsing Market.
Dow Jones Industrial Average Index

As it turned out, Main Street never missed a beat. In 1988 the economy continued to grow at a rapid rate, and the U.S. Fed was soon tightening again to rein in potential inflationary pressures. In short, for the real economy, the 1987 stock market crash proved to be a false alarm.

But the pattern had now been established. Financial market innovation, amidst benign real economy circumstances, led to a market upheaval and a rapid Fed rescue operation. And it all occurred alongside a relatively tame inflation backdrop. Minsky's framework was coming into focus.

Junk Bonds and the S&L Crisis: A Major Disruption Amidst Modest Inflation

If the portfolio insurance–driven 1987 crash was just a fire drill, the collapse of the Savings & Loan industry turned out to be the real deal. Before it was over, Fed policy makers were forced to slash overnight interest rates. And a Republican administration was forced to design and implement a multi-hundred-billion-dollar bailout to stabilize the U.S. financial system.

Mainstream analysts, focusing on inflation as the key perpetrator of economic instability, completely misdiagnosed the period. If you understood the work of Hyman Minsky, however, you were not fooled by tame price pressures. Junk bonds were the innovation du jour, and S&Ls, for the most part, were holding the black queen. As a recent enthusiast to Minsky's theories, I was compelled to forecast a wild round of interest rate ease and outright buying of damaged assets by the federal government. My forecast was on the money, and it gained me a fair amount of professional attention. It also precipitated a meeting that won me a very dear friend.

A Level Playing Field Levels the S&L Industry

How did the U.S. thrift industry invest its way into oblivion? Three miscalculations followed one after the other from the late 1970s through the late 1980s. Disintermediation, the early postwar problem for S&Ls, led to deregulation of the banking industry. With newfound powers, thrifts competed for money, using the proceeds to stock up on Wall Street's newest invention—junk bonds. When junk bonds hit a pothole, the S&L industry hit the skids.

What was disintermediation? From the 1950s through the 1970s, the S&L industry always lost deposits at the end of economic expansions. Regulation Q strictly limited the interest rate that thrifts could pay for their savings deposits. When interest rates rose, commercial banks raised their deposit and CD rates. But Regulation Q prevented thrifts from following suit, and money fled the S&Ls. The periodic flight from thrifts would force them to shut down their loan offices: if you are losing your deposits, you have less money to lend.[3]

In the early 1980s landmark banking industry deregulation was enacted. Regulation Q was abolished. This was supposed to create a level playing field, one in which thrifts could offer higher interest rates and compete for deposits. But a problem remained. S&Ls lent money to home buyers. Commercial banks lent money to risky companies and were able to charge higher interest rates. How could thrifts compete for funds if they could not afford to set up large commercial loan departments? Wall Street came to the rescue. Junk bonds were loans to risky companies, distributed by Wall Street. This *high-yield* paper seemed tailormade for thrifts. It provided a return that allowed S&Ls to compete, without requiring them to staff a commercial loan office.

Over the mid-1980s, thrifts became major buyers of junk bonds. They did so with little serious analysis of the underlying companies that offered up the bonds. A limited staff, after all, was a big part of the attraction. Wall Street, in theory, filled in the knowledge gap with high-yield research. But Wall Street, for the most part, was not holding the bonds. It was simply issuing them and collecting fees. This set up a moral hazard that invited excessive junk bond issuance.[4]

Were most of the companies in a position to honor their debts? In the mid-1980s, amidst low inflation and growing confidence in Fed policy, the conventional answer was yes. But that answer depended upon an extended period of good economic growth with low inflation and low interest rates.

The problem, of course, is that a promise of blue skies ahead is not a guarantee. We live in a world that once, last, and always is uncertain. Moreover, with junk bonds comprising a big chunk of thrift assets, the United States was set up for a Minsky moment. Recall that the critical Minsky observation is that risky finance sets the economy up for big disruptions from small disappointments. And so it was in the early 1990s.

Mainstream Economists and the 1990 Soft Landing That Wasn't

The widely held view in the late 1980s focused on climbing wage and price pressures. All eyes were on the U.S. Federal Reserve Board. The hope was that its stepwise increases for the Fed funds rate would slow U.S. activity and tame inflation without tipping the economy into recession. In the summer of 1990 nearly 90 percent of published forecasters were confident that the Fed would deliver a soft landing.[5]

In August 1990, however, the unexpected happened. Saddam Hussein invaded Kuwait. Oil prices soared. Long-term interest rates rose rapidly, and recession fears leapt. Conventional analysts acknowledged that the oil shock raised recession risks. But they also held out the hope that a quick war, and a speedy reversal for crude costs, would limit any downside.

As it turned out, the war lasted only a few days, and oil prices plunged, retracing their entire rise in a few short weeks. Mainstream analysts, in response, raised their expectations for economic growth. Indeed, Alan Greenspan, responding to a question during Congressional testimony in February 1990, suggested that second-half economic growth could turn out to be surprisingly robust. Consumer purchasing power had been restored, he noted, compliments of falling crude. A healthy second half, he mused, was a reasonable expectation.

Not Iraq and the Tanks, Debt and the Banks

As a Wall Street forecaster at the time, I saw it very differently. The Fed's decision to raise interest rates, to stem inflationary pressures, had destroyed the simple arithmetic that made junk bond investments reasonable. Initially Fed-engineered increases for short-term interest rates, put in place in 1988-1989, pushed junk company borrowing costs for short-term money substantially higher. In 1990, the economic weakness leading up to the Iraq War squeezed their businesses. One by one they began to default on their interest payments. Initially, S&Ls tried to sell the suspect parts of their junk bond portfolios. But soon enough it became a panic.

How do Wall Street fans of Hy define a Minsky moment? When you own risky assets that are falling in value and you need cash, you have to start selling your good risky assets. If everyone does this at the same time, the price of good risky assets begins to fall, and soon it looks like all risky assets are bad assets. That is the Minsky moment.

And so, in December 1990, with the world captivated by the imminent war in Iraq, I wrote a research paper entitled "Cash, at Long, Long Last, Is Trash" (see sidebar). The piece elevated the S&L crisis to center stage. A bankrupt thrift industry, it seemed clear to me, would prevent any reasonable rebound for housing. Therefore, the economy would struggle for an extended period. My all-encompassing one-liner for the Shearson Lehman sales force? "Not Iraq and the tanks, Debt and the Banks!" And the punch line for the forecast explained the research report's title. The Federal Reserve would not be tightening to contain rising inflationary pressures associated with the jump for oil prices. Instead we would witness dramatic Fed ease. The collapse for money market rates would force investors to move out of money market funds and into stocks and bonds. Thus, cash returns would become trash returns, to the benefit of stocks, bonds, and the economy.

CASH, AT LONG, LONG LAST, IS TRASH

Equity ownership, or a piece of the action, is the essence of the difference between capitalist-based economies and the planned economies of the Soviet Union, China, and, until recently, Eastern Europe. Yet the last three years have witnessed both the wholesale collapse of the economic and social structure of these planned economies and near universal disillusion with Wall Street, the most visible and dynamic capital market in the world. The irony of the 1980s, then, is that while communism failed, the free world's economic cornerstone fell into disrepute.

Our thesis for the 1990s reflects our belief that today's recession is finishing the work begun in the recessions of the early 1980s. Simply put, we believe that the coming U.S. expansion will be one that preserves the low inflation of the 1980s, but adds to it dramatically lower U.S. interest rates.

In turn, these lower rates will lift bond prices and catapult equity share prices to levels that will once again make equity the capital raising method of choice.

We believe that a substantial fall in both U.S. inflation and real short-term interest rates will meaningfully change investor attitudes about assets. The major fall for inflation recorded in the 1980s had undeniably positive effects on the prices of stocks and bonds. But super high real short rates translated into extraordinary returns on cash. As a consequence, U.S. households remained lukewarm about equity investments. With short rates now in the midst of a deep fall, many investors will be compelled to exit out of cash instruments and accept the inherent risks of bonds and stocks to garner the returns they are accustomed to.

In turn, substantially higher equity share prices will radically alter corporate finance arithmetic in the years directly ahead. The 1990s will be a decade in which capital is raised in the equity marketplace with the proceeds generally used to finance company investment and expansion plans. Such corporate finance pursuits will stand in stark contrast to the debt financed, stock buy-back, company constricting dynamic that ruled the 1980s. Investment bankers may never be thought of as "good deed doers," but in the 1990s, Wall Street's bad boy status should fade as equity-backed business activities rise.

In sum, we are contending that today's recession and debt decline, and yesterday's debt excess and corporate sector shrinkage, all can be explained as part of the decade-long process to unwind the great U.S. inflation of 1960-1980. Low inflation and low money market interest rates will redirect individuals in increasing numbers to equity ownership. U.S. corporations will raise funds in the equity marketplace and use the proceeds to expand plant and increase the workforces of their profitable businesses.

—Reprinted from Shearson Lehman Brothers,
November 5, 1990

When the research was distributed, a close friend reacted. "Your 'Cash Is Trash' assertion is vintage Minsky. Would you like to meet him?"

As I noted in this book's preface, I jumped at the offer, and a dinner was soon arranged.

At the meeting, Minsky outdid me. "Short rates will fall to 3 percent," he wagered. "This banking system will need enormous ease to restart the lending machine."

And so it went. By the fall of 1991 conventional economists had to change their tune. Alan Greenspan began talking about "secular headwinds" associated with debt excesses of the 1980s. Throughout 1992 and for much of 1993, economic growth was disappointing, and Fed ease kept on coming. Fed funds, as Minsky had guessed, bottomed at 3 percent. And the period of subpar growth had lasted for four years.

To my way of thinking, the Minsky model had triumphed. Amidst relatively tame inflation pressures, the accepted wisdom called for a quick economic rebound after a mild dose of interest rate ease. Instead, the economy struggled for four years, Fed ease turned out to be breathtaking, and an unprecedented bailout was needed to right the economic ship. Thus, a savvy analyst was now supposed to realize that Wall Street and the banks, not wages and prices, were the central drivers in the new business cycle. To the ultimate detriment of the overall economy, that insight remained elusive over the entirety of the next 18 years.

The onset of collapse in Japan, on the back of imploding asset prices, occurred roughly coincident with the 1990-1991 recession in the United States. The Asian contagion followed, in the mid-1990s. These back-to-back investment boom and bust experiences are the subject of the next chapter.

Chapter | 8

FINANCIAL MAYHEM IN ASIA: JAPAN'S IMPLOSION AND THE ASIAN CONTAGION

Speculative manias gather speed through expansion of money and credit . . .
—Charles Kindleberger, *Manias, Panics, and Crashes*, 1978

Three times in the past 20 years we have witnessed meteoric leaps for Asian asset markets that financed powerful investment booms. In two of three cases, in Japan in the early 1990s and in emerging Asia in the late 1990s, markets collapsed, banks flirted with insolvency, and deep and protracted recessions took hold. As these words go to print, China's investment boom is teetering following the collapse for Chinese share prices and the sharp falloff in money inflows from the developed world. If history is a guide, however, China's investment explosion and its heady growth rates are very much at risk.

Amidst the 2009 global downturn, the lessons that went unlearned from Asia's experiences deserve careful scrutiny. As we detail below, Japan's lost decade presses home the fact that risk taking by banks and other finance companies is essential for economic growth. Their timid initial attempts at bank recapitalization and the economywide risk aversion that took hold in postcollapse Japan are sobering reminders about the dangers immediately ahead. As we contemplate a way out of our current morass, we need to be mindful of the problems we may be creating for tomorrow.

Conversely, the more rapid return to recovery experienced by emerging Asian economies in the late 1990s reflected their ability to sharply reduce their collective debt burdens by exporting their way into solvency. Ironically, then, the easy money that financed the consumer spending boom in the United States from 1998 through 2005 played a central role in today's U.S. problems and yesterday's Asian salvation. It would be good now if countries like China, Russia, and Taiwan, which have built up massive foreign exchange reserves, were to boost their domestic demand and run current account deficits for a while. It would help moderate recession in the rest of the world.

From Japan Inc. to the Lost Decade

The extraordinary rise and collapse of everything to do with Japan occurred roughly coincident with the S&L crisis in the United States. But the magnitude of the Japanese financial system crisis dwarfed the S&L debacle and any other market upheaval since the Great Depression. As we detailed earlier, the U.S. problem in the early 1990s stemmed from the fact that many thrift institutions and banks had lent too much money to risky companies. When recession took hold, many of these companies looked shaky. The value of bank assets, therefore, had to be reduced. And banks, in need of additional capital, curtailed their lending.

Japan in the early 1990s faced the S&L problem on steroids. Japanese banks watched the value of their stock holdings fall by 65 percent. Their commercial real estate holdings fell by 80 percent. The land they owned fell by 80 percent as well. Even the value of golf memberships fell by 80 percent over the first half of the 1990s. Deposit insurance prevented massive runs on Japanese banks. But by early in the decade the world knew that Japan's banks, if forced to value assets at market prices, were bankrupt.

In response, Japanese banks curtailed lending and eked their way through the decade. Only massive government spending and strong exports kept the Japanese economy from plunging. When the decade concluded, a tally of the costs of the burst bubble made for grim reading. Incredibly, at the peak for the painfully tepid recovery that Japan managed later in the decade, industrial production, housing starts, and car sales were all lower than they were in 1989. Big government intervention and belated bank bailouts had prevented a depression in Japan, but the real economy costs of the burst asset bubble had been a lost decade in terms of economic growth.

A Focus on Trade and the Yen and a Fascination with Low Inflation

What did Japan do so terribly wrong? In the latter part of the 1980s, monetary policy stayed easy, ignoring the incomprehensible rise for the prices of any and all Japanese assets. At the peak, it was estimated that the land around the emperor's palace in Tokyo was equal to the value of all the land in the state of California! The shares of Japanese car makers reached values that suggested these companies were infinitely more valuable than their equally savvy German counterparts. The overall stock market, after logging in five strong years, doubled in value in the three years leading up to its early 1990 peak. Quite simply, it was Tulips in Tokyo. How could Japanese central bankers have ignored such insanity? Japan's policy makers in the 1980s, like their U.S. counterparts, focused on real economy fundamentals and ignored asset markets. And the widely held view was that Japan was in the driver's seat. Japan's boom in the early and mid-1980s was export driven. They were, in particular, extraordinarily successful exporters to the United States, wreaking havoc on U.S. manufacturing company markets and profits. By the mid-1980s, Ezra Vogel's book *Japan as No. 1: Lessons for America* was required reading in Washington circles.

Here is a popular joke from 1987 that captured the sense of inevitable Japanese triumph:

On a flight over the Pacific the captain announces that passengers must reduce the plane's weight by 10,000 pounds or a deadly crash will be inevitable. With nothing left to jettison, and still 600 pounds too heavy, the captain asks for three volunteers to sacrifice themselves and leap to their death. The first declares, "They'll always be an England!" and jumps. The second yells out, "Vivre la France!" and leaps. The third, a Japanese businessman, approaches the open door, then turns and explains, "Before I jump I want to speak for just a moment about Japanese management practices." An American businessman quickly pushes him aside. As he readies himself to leap, he explains, "I'd rather jump than listen to another speech about Japanese business practices."

Japan, it seemed clear, was destined to become the world's number one economic powerhouse. Climbing asset markets simply validated that opinion. The Bank of Japan ignored them. Taking a cue from their western counterparts, they celebrated minimal wage and price inflation, targeted very low interest rates, and fed a multiyear boom. As they saw it, tame price pressures and limited wage increases translated to limited excesses.

Japan's policy makers did focus on their very large and politically embarrassing trade surplus. Easy money, they believed, would keep spending strong and help to increase Japanese imports. Thus, their focus on trade and their comfort level with very low inflation justified— so far as they could see—super low interest rates in the face of a wild rise for any and every asset price.

The super easy monetary policy led to very low long-term rates in Japan. This provided global stock market strategists with some comfort when they confronted the sky-high price for the Nikkei. I had occasion to be subjected to this in Asia, at the government of Singapore's Global Investment Prospects Conference in the summer of 1989. I was the keynote speaker on the U.S. situation. I was preceded by a strategist from London, who was bullish on Japanese stocks. At the time, the Nikkei had climbed to an improbable height relative to most other stock markets around the world (see Figure 8.1). But the London guru had a key slide that he referred to at least a dozen times as he tried to calm global investors who were nervous about super expensive Japanese equities. "Look at how low long rates are in Japan," he said again and again. "Japanese stocks aren't expensive. They reflect the reality of super low long rates in the Japanese economy."

I spoke next on the U.S. economy. When I took questions, oddly enough, the first issue I was asked about was Japan, not the United

Figure 8.1

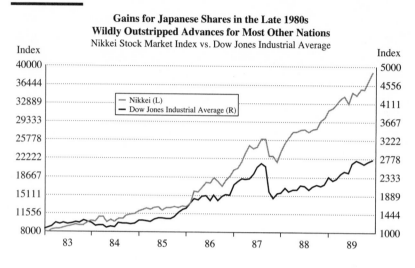

Gains for Japanese Shares in the Late 1980s
Wildly Outstripped Advances for Most Other Nations
Nikkei Stock Market Index vs. Dow Jones Industrial Average

States: "What do you think about the argument that Japanese stocks are not expensive because of the low bond yields sported in Japan?" Before I could censure myself, I responded, "That's easy. I think the Japanese bond market is as crazy as the Japanese stock market."

Over the next year, the Japanese bond market came under pressure as a rise in inflation forced the Bank of Japan to raise interest rates. Tight money popped the Japanese bubble, and the Japanese equity market fell by nearly 66 percent over the next five years.[1] Simply put, by keeping its interest rates low, the Bank of Japan fed the boom in assets for half a decade. The Bank of Japan accepted the conventional wisdom and ignored asset markets. When credit conditions were tightened in response to rising price pressures, the Bank of Japan oversaw an asset market collapse that paralleled the one in the United States in the 1930s. The Japanese economy, feared as a rival to the United States in the late 1980s, receded into near obscurity over the next 10 years (see Figure 8.2).

Figure 8.2

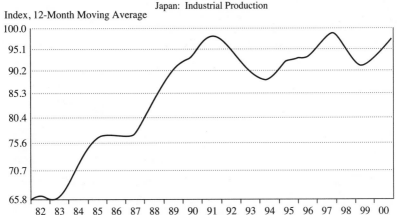

Japan's Lost Decade: Production Was Lower in 2000 Than It Was in 1990

Japan: Industrial Production

East Asia's Miracle Goes Bust, and Booming U.S. Consumers Come to the Rescue

In the latter half of the 1990s, boom times unfolded in emerging Asian economies. And the booms were initially sensible, reflecting sound investment opportunities. The dynamics were straightforward. The collapse of the former Soviet Union and China's newfound willingness to interact with capitalist nations supercharged trade and capital flows between the developed world and emerging Asian economies. Cheap and dependable labor, if married to twenty-first-century machinery, promised highly competitive companies.

The developed world, excited about participating in these markets, poured dollars in. Emerging Asian countries boomed. Their currencies soared. Their banks and industrial companies took on large debts. They borrowed money, mostly in dollars. Their assets, of course, were in their host countries and therefore valued in local currencies. In the end, that currency mismatch—borrowing in dollars and earning money in Thai baht or Korean won—would turn a cyclical downturn into a major Asian financial crisis.

Again, however, it was financial system dynamics, not wage and price pressures, that were the forces for instability. In this case, Asian central banks were only partially to blame. The developed world was the primary source of easy money in emerging Asia. In that sense, Asian economies suffered, in large part, for our sins.[2]

What went wrong in emerging Asia? Paul Krugman had the goods on the situation early on. The powerful growth rates that these countries sported reflected the boom that comes when you replace a handsaw with a lathe. By giving Asian workers more machines—capital deepening—their productivity rose rapidly, supporting rapid economic growth rates.

But, as Krugman pointed out, once these workers had state-of-the-art machines, subsequent Asian economy growth rates would begin to look like those of the developed world. And slower growth, he went on to say, was not what investors in East Asian companies were betting on. Moreover, profits are high when capital can be employed along with skilled and cheap labor. But as the capital-to-labor ratio rises, the rate of profit can be expected to fall. The gain from adding still more capital equipment is less than it was for the first injection.

Expectations that rapid investment could be permanently associated with high rates of profit depended on the belief that the Asian economies had discovered some elixir that would keep profits high indefinitely. As usual in a boom, many commentators persuaded themselves that it was so, that a peculiarly Asian form of technological progress would sustain the boom. Krugman saw no evidence for that belief. It appeared that the growth could be explained by the investment. There was no magic ingredient of unusual technical advance that would keep profits booming.

As Krugman anticipated, slower growth rates began to appear. Once they did, rearview mirror investors began to dump Asian stocks. And at that point, their capital market problems became a currency crisis. Recall that Asian miracle growth rates led companies to borrow in dollars and earn money in Asian currencies. What happens when your debts are in dollars, and the dollar jumps versus your currency? The level of your debt—valued in your currency—leaps relative to the value of your earnings. Once again we find ourselves discovering an adverse feedback loop, which delivered a powerful blow to many countries' economies and was largely independent of wage and price inflation dynamics (see Figure 8.3).

Figure 8.3

In 1997, Fading Confidence in the Asian Miracle
Weighed First on Stock Markets
Korea: Kospi Index

The financial difficulties in Asia stemmed primarily from the questionable borrowing and lending practices of banks and finance companies in the troubled Asian currencies. Companies in Asia tend to rely more on bank borrowing to raise capital than on issuing bonds or stock.... International borrowing involves two other types of risk. The first is in the maturity distribution of accounts. The other is whether the debt is private or sovereign. As for maturity distribution, many banks and businesses in the troubled Asian economies appear to have borrowed short-term for longer-term projects.... Mostly... these short-term loans have fallen due before projects are operational or before they are generating enough profits to enable repayments to be made, particularly if they go into real estate development.... As long as an economy is growing and not facing particular financial difficulties... obtaining new loans as existing ones mature may not be particularly difficult.... When a financial crisis hits, however, loans suddenly become more difficult to procure, and lenders may decline to refinance debts. Private-sector financing virtually evaporates for a time.

Currency depreciation, in turn, places an additional burden on local borrowers whose debts are denominated in dollars. They now are faced with debt service costs that have risen in proportion to the currency depreciation.... In the South Korean case, for example, the drop in the value of the won from 886 to 1,701 won per dollar between July 2 and December 31, 1997, nearly doubled the repayment bill when calculated in won for Korea's foreign debts.

—"The 1997-1998 Asian Financial Crisis,"
Dick Nanto, Congressional Research Service, February 6, 1998

The East Asian crisis was not a bubble of the proportions of Japan in the 1980s or the technology bubble in the United States in the 1990s. Indeed, in this case you could argue that the bust was as much an example of excess as the boom had been.

Trouble started in Thailand when the Thai baht came under pressure. The government went through $33 billion of foreign exchange reserves before deciding to let the currency float down. But once that currency depreciated, alarm quickly replaced optimism. The Philippines, Malaysia, and Indonesia were all forced off currency pegs. That created a negative feedback—the prospect of rising interest rates to defend currencies sent stock markets into another tailspin. The Korean won then came under pressure—with some justification, since Korean institutions had borrowed in dollars to make property loans that paid rents in won. But thereafter most Asian currencies came under speculative attack not as the result of a careful calculation of the prospects for each economy but as a result of generalized fear (see Figure 8.4).

Runs on the currencies sent countries scurrying to the IMF for balance-of-payments support loans to tide them over. The IMF signed agreements with Thailand, Indonesia, and South Korea, while Malaysia and Hong Kong found their own ways out of the crisis, in

Figure 8.4

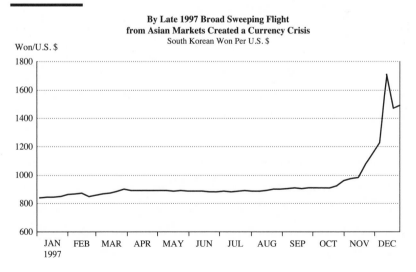

**By Late 1997 Broad Sweeping Flight
from Asian Markets Created a Currency Crisis**
South Korean Won Per U.S. $

the one case imposing capital controls and in the other aggressively supporting not only the currency but the stock market too. Those measures worked, though there were loud protestations at the time from the orthodox.

Elsewhere, the IMF prescription—devaluation and fiscal stringency, cutting back on spending and raising taxes—was widely applied. The medicine worked, but only because the rest of the non-Asian world was in a robust state. The Asian countries were a small enough part of the world economy to be able to take the hit to domestic demand and export their way to recovery.

Once again it was a case of an investment boom that went to excess fueled by easy money and financial market dynamics. When the boom went bust, the rain fell on both the just and the unjust, as investors sold indiscriminately. The penalty to the real economy dwarfed the costs that economists—focused on wages and prices—expected. Drops in both currencies and stock markets were severe. In Thailand they were down 38 and 26 percent respectively, in South Korea by 50 and 30 percent, and in Indonesia by 81 and 40 percent.

As smallish economies with heavy reliance on exports, the Asians were able to recover by increasing sales to the rest of the world. And they resolved never again to fall into such a situation and be beholden to the IMF and its austerity policies. Accordingly, they determined to keep their exchange rates low and to stay ultracompetitive in export markets.

The 2009 crisis, unfortunately, is widespread, affecting the great majority of the economies of the world. Thus, the recovery forged by Asian economies offers no real guidelines. By definition, everyone cannot drive currencies lower and exports higher. Attempts to do this would be "beggar my neighbor policies" that would worsen the situation. Likewise, austerity—cutting back on government-financed spending—would only worsen the global recession. We have to learn the lessons of history—but the right lessons. On that score, the late 2008 commitment to ramp up government spending in China, the United States, and most of Europe has to be looked at as good news. Even German policy makers, notorious for their conservatism on economic matters, acknowledged that austerity makes little sense amidst deep global retrenchment.

Chapter | 9

THE BRAVE-NEW-WORLD BOOM GOES BUST: THE 1990s TECHNOLOGY BUBBLE

What happens, basically, is that some event changes the economic outlook. New opportunities for profit are seized, and overdone, in ways so closely resembling irrationality as to constitute a mania.
—Charles Kindleberger, *Manias, Panics, and Crashes*, 1978

In the late 1980s risky finance collided with rising interest rates. The late 1990s brought us a wild asset bubble, pure and simple. As I have emphasized on several occasions, you don't need "the madness of crowds" to generate a Minsky moment. Expectations in the late 1980s were not excessive—debt use was. The period leading up to the end of the millennium, in stark contrast, *was* downright crazy. As I admit to late in this chapter, near the end it was nutty enough to drive me into therapy. Indeed, if I were a speculating type, I would have lost the ranch sometime in the autumn of 1999. When the bubble burst and technology shares plunged, my initial reaction was relief. Thank God, I thought, I'm not crazy after all.

Like nearly all of the investment bubbles throughout history, the 1990s episode had legitimate underpinnings. For one, even the most skeptical investors were forced to acknowledge that inflation had been vanquished. The moderate inflation, in place in the middle 1990s, gave way to readings of less than 2 percent in 1998, taking us back to levels not seen since the early 1960s. Second, and probably more important, the demise of the Soviet Union delivered a peace dividend to the United States and the world. Defense spending, a waste at best, fell sharply, and moot cold war dictates cleared away major impediments to doing business in Latin America, Eastern Europe, and Asia. Finally, and most visibly, telephone/computer connectivity began to pay healthy dividends to the U.S. economy. These developments combined to deliver an unmistakable jump in U.S. productivity performance. Faster economic growth alongside low inflation was very good news, pure and simple.

As I emphasized earlier in this book, one of the virtues of free market capitalism is that it rewards success. And in the early and mid-1990s, the many innovations that technology companies delivered drove investment dollars into the information industry, replicating and expanding upon these successes. But history tells us that at the end of the movie, success breeds excess. And it is hard to find a period in the world's history when that was as true as it was for technology share prices in the late 1990s.

Bubble Formation

From spring 1997 through spring 2000, the fascination with new age notions became intense and concentrated. Overwhelming attention was given to technology companies. In late 1998 through early 2000, tech stocks continued to soar, even as most of the rest of the stock market was in retreat, in response to the stepwise tightening Fed policy makers had embarked upon. Belief in a brave new world, driven by technology innovations, had taken hold. When I began to warn that technology stocks were at prices impossible to justify, I was often treated to the smile that is usually reserved for small children and benign idiots. Others were more direct: "Come on, Bob, get with the program. This time it's different."

Robert Shiller in his excellent book *Irrational Exuberance* documented the many ways in which a herd mentality took over in the U.S. stock market. He also provided a few straightforward measures of stock market value in order to demonstrate just how out of whack late 1990s technology share prices were relative to the broad sweep of capital markets' history. He emphasized that a low P/E ratio, more times than not over the past century, was a sign that future equity market gains would be above average. Shiller's point was obvious. The late 1990s record P/E ratios were a potent portent of bad things to come (see Figure 9.1). Shiller's excellent work, however, failed to explicitly address the claim that things were fundamentally *different*. Thus, his book, published on the eve of the collapse in technology shares, was roundly dismissed by any and all who had drunk the Kool-Aid. From their perspective, he just did not get it.

I had the misfortune to experience this sentiment firsthand, at the White House Conference on the New Economy, in April 2000. As I noted earlier, Alan Greenspan was the rock star at the conference, peopled almost entirely by true believers. Somewhat inexplicably, I was also in attendance. After the main session was held, all participants were assigned to breakout groups. I joined about a dozen others. Our collective task was to answer the question: "What could go wrong?"

Not being the shy type, I volunteered within the first five minutes of our round table that the obvious issue we had to grapple with was the potential for a bursting of the large technology share price bubble.

Figure 9.1

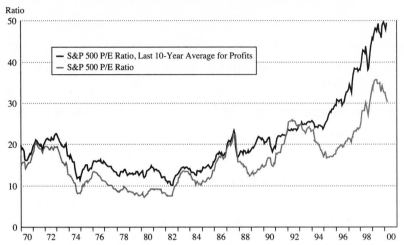

P/E Ratios Are Extreme.
Use 10-Year Smoothing on Profits and They Look Insane.

Our moderator, a White House insider whose name, thankfully, I do not remember, pounced: "This is not a bubble!"

I looked at the others; they looked down at their shoes. And for the remainder of the two hours the group exchanged pleasantries. In the end the group decided that the big risk going forward, in this brave new world, was the technology gap that was sure to worsen between the United States and poor African and Latin American nations. Bubble? The word never was uttered again.

Not Highly Unlikely, Mathematically Impossible

Fresh from the White House meeting, I was now a man on a mission. Shiller's book, I had previously thought, made it impossible to deny the bubble in technology share prices. Now I understood that to deflect the arguments of the true believers, you had to be able to replace "highly unlikely" with "mathematically impossible." By spring 2000 the situation was so crazy that it took less than a week to construct the case. As I wrote at that time, "Perhaps the most astounding aspect of the February peak for the U.S. equity market was that the implied economic future embedded in February share prices was not unlikely. It was impossible."

At this point, I imagine some readers are crying, "Foul!" After all, a central tenet of this book is that when it comes to the future, nobody knows for sure! True enough. But in April 2000, I was not declaring that I was certain I knew what was going to happen. I simply knew that the vision of the future embedded in technology share prices that spring could not possibly happen. There was, in fact, no way for technology company earnings to grow at the rate analysts were projecting. It was not unlikely, it was impossible.

Ironically, it was Greenspan's White House speech that put me on the trail. His enthusiasm for the new economy included these words:

> While growth in companies' projected earnings has been revised up almost continuously across many sectors of the economy in recent years, the gap in expected profit growth between technology firms and others has persistently widened. As a result, security analysts' projected five-year growth of earnings for technology companies now stands nearly double that for the remaining S&P 500 firms.
>
> To the extent that there is an element of prescience in these expectations, it would reinforce the notion that technology synergies are still expanding and that expectations of productivity growth are still rising. There are many who argue, of course, that it is not prescience but wishful thinking. History will judge.

There it was, the Holy Grail! The analysts who covered tech stocks believed that long-term earnings growth for their stocks, on average, would double the growth registered by other companies. A quick collection of long-term earnings forecasts for the top 20 technology companies in the S&P revealed that taken together, technology company earnings were expected to grow at a 22 percent per year rate for at least another five years (see Table 9.1). Most analysts in fact agreed that long-term growth could be taken to mean 10 years. Get out your calculator, plug in a 22 percent growth rate for tech earnings for 10 years, and it turns out that technology companies, in 2010, would have captured 21 percent of projected U.S. corporate earnings, up from 4.5 percent in 2000. Again, that was not unlikely, it was impossible.[1]

The Boom Goes Bust and There's Panic in the Air

It would be very impressive if I could claim that my impossibility theorem, laid alongside excellent works done by people like Robert Shiller, played a role in bursting the late 1990s technology bubble. It simply is not true. Naysayers swam against a tide of enthusiasm for years. I had, embarrassingly, been warning of stock market excesses for more than a year. Shiller, a critic with much more stature, had met with the Federal Reserve Board to warn of a growing equity market bubble—in December 1996!

The bubble continued to expand, in part, because easy money was forthcoming from the Federal Reserve. A change in heart at the Fed, and a bout of aggressive tightening, burst the bubble. As it turned out, tight money arrived in early 2000, around the time of Shiller's book and coincident with my small contribution to the argument. But make

Table 9.1

Too Good to Be True

Companies*	Long-Term Annual Growth (%)	EPS Trailing 12-Months ($)	Shares Outstanding (In Billions)	Earnings Trailing 12-Months (In $s Billions)	Earnings 2010 Trailing 12-Months (In $s Billions)
1 Cisco Systems (CSCO)	30	0.44	6.9	3.05	42.08
2 Microsoft (MSFT)	25	1.60	5.2	8.33	77.55
3 Intel (INTC)	20	2.32	3.3	7.75	48.01
4 Oracle (ORCL)	25	0.56	2.8	1.58	14.71
5 Int Business Machines (IBM)	14	3.71	1.8	6.66	24.67
6 Lucent Technologies (LU)	20	1.12	3.2	3.57	22.1
7 Nortel Networks (NT)	21	1.28	1.4	1.76	11.86
8 America Online (AOL)	50	0.27	2.3	0.62	35.51
9 Sun Microsystems (SUNW)	21	0.79	1.6	1.25	8.41
10 Dell Computer (DELL)	33	0.69	2.6	1.77	30.65
11 Hewlett-Packard (HWP)	15	3.09	1.0	3.09	12.5
12 EMC (EMC)	31	1.11	1.0	1.15	17.12
13 Texas Instruments (TXN)	24	1.83	0.8	1.49	12.8
14 Qualcomm (QCOM)	38	0.77	0.7	0.54	13.6
15 Motorola (MOT)	19	2.07	0.7	1.48	8.42
16 Yahoo! (YHOO)	56	0.27	0.5	0.14	12.12
17 Applied Materials (AMAT)	24	1.29	0.8	0.99	8.54
18 Veritas Software (VRTS)	49	0.36	0.4	0.14	7.47
19 Compaq Computer (CPQ)	19	0.29	1.7	0.49	2.81
20 Computer Associates (CA)	18	2.64	0.6	1.55	8.12
Total				47.4	419.06

*S&P 500 members by market capitalization weight

no mistake about it, in the spring of 2000 it was tight money, not troubling math, that burst the fantastic technology share price bubble. In the early months of 2000, the Fed raised rates by twice as much as normal, letting the world know that it had every intention of imposing a break in the boom. What prompted the Fed's move to raise rates at an accelerating pace? Its boilerplate explanation read as follows:

> Increases in demand have remained in excess of even the rapid pace of productivity-driven gains in potential supply, exerting continued pressure on resources. The Committee is concerned that this disparity in the growth of demand and potential supply will continue, which could foster inflationary imbalances that would undermine the economy's outstanding performance.

More simply, it judged the economy to be growing too rapidly, threatening an unhealthy rise for price pressures. The CPI's climb had accelerated from 2 to 3 percent over the previous year. Fed policy makers, at least officially, were simply responding to their number one worry, climbing inflation. In commentary published years later it is clear that Fed officials recognized that stock prices were increasingly impossible to justify. It may be that they *inflated* their concern about the uptick for price pressures in the face of the impossible to ignore equity market bubble. But by that time the damage was already done. A wild asset bubble had been left unattended, a consequence of a central bank policy that deemed wage and price excesses the key destabilizing forces. The 50 basis point squeeze in May 2000, with the threat of more to come, popped the technology share price bubble. And as almost everyone in the world now knows, once a speculative fever is broken, the selling can build to an equally breathtaking frenzy.

The swoon for tech shares was awe-inspiring. In its middle stages, with Nasdaq down by over 40 percent, I asked a respected colleague and kindred spirit how far he thought tech stocks could fall. "I'm 65 years old. I was there for the late 1960s run. At the peak everyone knows you have to own growth companies. And tech grows the fastest, so it's tech, tech, tech. By the time you bottom, people only want value, and technology companies, everyone agrees, offer next to no value—after all, in the end another company with a better widget always puts them out of business."

"You didn't answer my question," I said. "How far can they fall?"

"Simple. Use the square root rule. Look at the company's peak share price. Take the square root. When it hits that level, it's a buy."

Of course I thought he was kidding. But the truth is, that was about right. Cisco Systems peaked in 2000 at $81 a share. Its 2003 low? You guessed it, a little less than $9 a share.

Misguided Focus on Low Inflation Led to Confidence in Soft Landing

The technology bubble was the main event over the 1996-2003 period. Nevertheless, most economic forecasters ignored the deflationary power of falling asset markets. The adverse feedback loop that attends Minsky moments was the focus of only a short list of economists. In fact, the vast majority of forecasters denied recession risk in the United States until the gut-wrenching events of 9/11. That tragedy was the worst moment in the lives of most Americans of my generation. But the economic retrenchment that gripped the country had started nearly a year before. And it reflected the swoon for technology stocks. In the first weeks of 2001, I had parted company with the conventional wisdom:

> Nasdaq, we believe, was the central character in the drama that characterized U.S. economic performance over the past two years. Nevertheless, most economic forecasters cast Nasdaq with, at best, a supporting role. Given little inflation and visible Fed ease, those not focused on technology are able to minimize the risk of U.S. recession. We are compelled to claim that recession has taken hold because we think the boom and swoon for Nasdaq share prices is being echoed in the real economy. Explosive growth in technology investment was the real-side complement to the explosive rise in technology share prices. Booming consumer spending also owed much to the technology share price boom. With the bursting of the technology share price bubble now a reality, we see a slide for the real economy as inevitable.

Over the next two and a half years the U.S. economy languished. The jobless rate rose. The Fed kept easing. Inflation disappeared. And the stock market kept falling. By late October 2002 the equity market had been falling for 27 months, and the Fed had lowered overnight interest rates to 1 percent. None of this had anything to do with the destabilizing consequences of a rise for inflation. A growing asset bubble had been left unattended for years, and the 2001 recession reflected the failure to respond to that mushrooming excess.

Why did the Fed ignore the technology bubble? Unquestionably its central error was the singular attention it paid to wages and prices. In addition, however, in the late 1990s Greenspan and his colleagues confronted a world that had deep economic troubles. As I discuss in the next chapter, a charitable explanation for easy money into mid-1999 was that it was, in part, in reaction to the brutal bust that gripped much of Asia in 1998.

The lessons of the 1985-2000 period that should have taken hold as the new millennium began were twofold. Central bankers need to pay attention to asset prices. In addition, they need to recognize that asset prices are greatly influenced by global capital flows. In effect, we were now in global Minsky model territory. But the lessons went unheeded. And as the next chapter details, a truly global Minsky crisis turned out to be the end game for the succession of asset market excesses that began in the mid-1980s.

Hindsight Is 20/20

No serious analyst today disputes that the late 1990s technology stock run was anything but a wild bout of irrational exuberance. But if you lived through it, and you called the thesis into question at the time, it was a very painful period. I began warning clients about the risk of a bubble in early 1999. Six months later, with technology share prices still rocketing ahead, I felt beaten down. As we approached the new millennium, I went so far as to spend a few sessions with a local shrink. I needed a third party to judge whether I was letting my ego get in the way of the facts on the ground. The brave-new-world case all seemed increasingly preposterous to me. But it just isn't any fun playing the role of party pooper. What follows is a piece I wrote on the eve of the collapse of Nasdaq, in the spring of 2000.[2]

DEAR DR. FREUD . . .

Thanks, Doc, for seeing me on such short notice. I guess I should confess at the outset that I've never done this before; Italians traditionally go to confession. But I figure if Tony Soprano can whine about the emotional stress he feels as he blows people's brains out, then I can bend your ear about anxieties I have been feeling as a Wall Street "talking head."

For nearly 20 years, Doc, I figured I had the best job in the world. I get paid for staying on top of what's happening around the globe, and for declaring, once in a while, that I see important change on the horizon. It's hard to describe exactly how I come by my views. I read a great deal, I pore over data, and I talk, nearly nonstop, with clients about the world around us. Being highly compensated for staying well-informed and venturing forth with opinions, as far as I was concerned, was the best-of-all-possible jobs.

Until now! You see, Doc, all of a sudden I'm trapped by the images I see when I gaze into my crystal ball. The best part of my job is when the light bulb goes off above my head, and it dawns on me that the world is about to change. That's when I weave together a story about how tomorrow will be different, and I speculate about how investors can position themselves for what's on the horizon. Whether standing at a podium, sitting in a conference room, or cradling a telephone, I'm invigorated as my logic and enthusiasm capture my colleagues' attention. And if, over the ensuing quarters, my guesswork proves prescient, then I get the exhilaration of having been right about the changes that arrived on the economic scene.

But, Doc, what do you do if you don't like what you see? Worse, what do you do if your image of the future is retrograde, old school, and ugly, and it stands in stark contrast to an overwhelmingly wonderful *brave-new-world*-of-the-here-and-now?

What do I do, Doc, if my vision casts me in the role of Cassandra? There I am, at the podium, weaving my web, waving my wand, working my magic in an effort to win the audience over. But, who in their right mind would want to convince a group of his peers that things are not really that different, and that old fears are indeed well-founded?

And, Doc, I wish. Oh, how I wish I could believe. Life would be wonderful for me now if my crystal ball conjured up a picture of enduring perfection.

Let's face it, Doc, it may be me that lacks the vision. I just didn't have the foresight to quit college, start a firm, and earn $250 million before I was 30. I got a Ph.D., taught at MIT, worked in Washington and on Wall Street, and, at almost 50, I've discovered that I've been in the slow lane for all these years! So, who knows, maybe the dark color of my crystal ball is nothing more than the reflected hue of sour grapes.

Maybe a short list of soaring shares and a surge in margin debt and a grimacing Fed Chairman are all irrelevant. Maybe the old rules are for people like me, old fools. . . .

But, Doc. Doc, when I wake in the middle of the night, my nightmare is always the same. It's Lucy, Doc. And, I'm Charlie Brown. It's Lucy. She's holding the football. She's promised everyone that this time she won't pull it away. And, she told the truth, Doc, to everyone else.

She purrs that I'm the last to believe that in the new world, things can be counted on to be better than expected. Come on, she says, don't be the only one who hasn't shed his anxieties.

She wants me, Doc. Me. As the Charlie Brown of Wall Street, she wants me to conquer my fear. She wants me to run, pell-mell, toward the football she balances below her finger. She wants me, in full stride to unabashedly kick the football through the uprights and join the crowd of believers. And I hem, Doc, and I haw. And, I twist and turn. But the crowd grows more restless, and her gaze is enticing, and I want oh so much to be one with the happy campers, back amid the bullish who believe. And, so I go, I run, I do it, full speed, no fear, it's only right, why be a doubting Thomas. And, so I swing my leg, full-out, and almost see the ball splitting the uprights as it soars in the air.

But, no. My leg swings harmlessly through empty space. Lucy cackles, football in hand. The crowd has disappeared. She's laughing as I lay on my behind.

And there I lay, and then I mumble, Doc, I mumble. It's always the same, I just mumble, quietly mumble, "But, Lucy, you promised that it would be different this time."

Part | III

EMERGING REALITIES: 2007-2008

Chapter | 10

GREENSPAN'S CONUNDRUM FOSTERS THE HOUSING BUBBLE

You got to be careful if you don't know where you're going, because you might not get there.

—Yogi Berra

Most commentators argue that the seeds of the 2008 upheaval are to be found in the U.S. housing market. I certainly agree that the immediate causes of the crisis were made in the U.S.A. Wall Street "innovation" delivered us new ways to borrow in order to buy a home, and these mortgages, we now know, had serious flaws. Mortgage originators collapsed borrowing standards, leaving the housing financing market with absolutely no *margin of safety*. The entire architecture of mortgage finance, it's now perfectly clear, depended upon an unending rise for home prices. And the long-standing Greenspan refusal to react to asset prices kept money easy and inflated the game, worsening both the bubble and the bust.

But access to easy mortgage money in the United States and many other developed world housing markets began in the late 1990s. Low interest rates throughout much of the developed world were an important part of the rescue operation for Asia, following the currency crises and deep recessions that gripped many Pacific Basin nations. In the pages that follow, therefore, we start not in 2005 but in 1998.

The 1998 Ease: Greenspan Saves the World?

Monetary policy in the late 1990s was just too easy. It nurtured the technology share price bubble into early 2000. The collapse for technology stocks, through much of 2002, in turn required a major dose of easy money. Clearly, the big ease in 2001-2003 played a key role in creating the next bubble—this time in the U.S. housing market.

But the world outside of the United States in the late 1990s was marching to a very different drum. As we detailed in Chapter 8, crisis took hold in many emerging Asian economies. Their distress infected U.S. financial markets. The Fed chose to ease interest rates in the fall of 1998, in direct response to the Long-Term Capital Management crisis. But the precipitating event that resulted in the LTCM panic was Russia's default. Clearly, U.S. monetary policy was responding to U.S. concerns, but global dynamics were key drivers.

Moreover, the green light that allowed Fed officials to stay easy in the late 1990s was low inflation. Careful analysis, today, reveals that it was the rest-of-world bust, not the brave-new-world boom, that explained the implausibly good inflation news of the period. Recall that from mid-1996 through mid-1999 the U.S. economy boomed, the unemployment rate fell to lows not seen since the early 1960s, *and U.S. inflation fell.* New economy enthusiasts attributed the good news to the powers of the computer and the cell phone, and envisioned an extended period of serenity.

A more sober look at the data supports a less inspiring explanation. Asia's collapse in 1997-1998 drove the dollar price of almost anything that traveled on a boat sharply lower. What happened? Deep Asian recessions cut the global demand for raw materials and for oil. Plunging Asian currencies drove the dollar prices of consumer manufactured goods down.

From the U.S. Fed's perspective, however, the whys and the wherefores were not important. Inflation was low, and share prices were not on their radar screen. Fed policy stayed easy amidst the U.S. economic boom.

As far as Asia was concerned, the easy-money-stoked boom for U.S. housing and consumer spending was music to their ears. In 1999, at a Congressional hearing on the U.S. trade deficit, I put it this way:

> The U.S. Fed and the U.S. consumer deserve medals for their performance over the 1998-1999 period. Asia's collapse could well have triggered a global deflationary bust, but for the timely and aggressive ease of the U.S. Fed last year. . . .
>
> Going forward, the newly emerging reality of rest-of-world recovery ends the need for booming U.S. spending. Moreover, the U.S. would be wise to steer a course aimed at slowing deficit growth, given the large and rapidly growing U.S. need for foreign capital inflows to finance this imbalance.[1]

As it turned out, low inflation, like almost everything else in the world at that time, was mostly made in Asia. Combine low inflation with easy Fed policy and falling Asian access to investment funds and we have an explanation for an unusual circumstance: very low mortgage rates in a booming U.S. economy. Much of the strength for housing and consumer spending in 1997-2000 was a consequence of the bust that enveloped emerging Asia.

The 2001 Brave-New-World Bust Fails to Lay a Glove on Housing

As I noted above, it was unusual for mortgage rates to remain low late in an economic expansion. In the boom and bust cycles of the 1960s and 1970s, housing booms occurred in the first few years of a recovery. As the expansion ages, interest rates tend to rise. A spike for inflation and interest rates is the catalyst for recession. And housing investment, without exception, plunges (Figure 10.1).

Figure 10.1

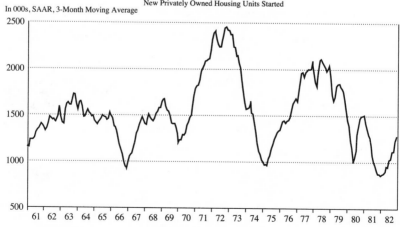

Housing Activity Plunged in Every Recession, 1961-1982
New Privately Owned Housing Units Started

In 000s, SAAR, 3-Month Moving Average

This did not occur, however, in the recession of 2001.

A short-lived bout of aggressive Fed tightening in early 2000 elicited a modest jump for long-term interest rates and a six-month pullback for housing starts. By late 2000 it became clear to the world that plunging technology share prices were ending the investment-led boom of the 1990s. Aggressive interest rate ease by the Fed, starting in the first week of 2001, encouraged a falling interest rate regime that lasted for nearly three years. By the end of that easing process, interest rates—including and especially mortgage rates—had fallen to levels not seen in a generation. Housing has always been the most interest-sensitive sector of the U.S. economy. Over the 2001-2003 period, housing failed to fall much and then began to rise with powerful momentum. The U.S. housing market simply skipped the recession of 2001(Figure 10.2).

Figure 10.2

Housing Activity Ignored the 2001 Recession
New Privately Owned Housing Units Started

Greenspan's Conundrum: The Fed Tightens and Asia Keeps Market Rates Low

The collapse for technology investment and the quick recession that took hold explain the persistence of low mortgage rates and the relatively healthy performance for housing in the 2001-2003 period. The housing boom, however, was just getting started.

The early years of the expansion ushered in the concept of the China price. In the late 1990s low U.S. inflation reflected the collapse of many Asian economies. The fantastic rise in exports from China to the United States, 2002-2004, delivered an avalanche of super-low-priced consumer goods. Core consumer goods prices in the United States actually fell sharply in 2003 for the first time on record (see Figure 10.3). Fed policy makers, blinded by low core inflation, kept interest rates extremely low throughout 2003. Only after it was clear that the Bush tax cuts had put the U.S. economy into high gear did Fed policy makers begin to raise interest rates.

Figure 10.3

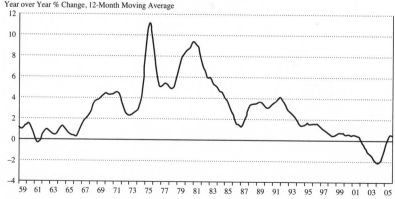

The China Price: U.S. Consumer Goods
Prices in Sharp Retreat, 2002-2004
Consumer Price Index, Commodities Less Food and Energy Commodities

The Fed began lifting the Fed funds rate in April of 2004. From a low of 1 percent, it raised Fed funds by 25 basis points. The Fed soon made it clear that it was its intention to slowly raise the Fed funds rate. Given the low inflation backdrop, it saw no need to quickly remove the stimulus that low interest rates provide.

Much of this book is concerned with the logical flaw that led the Fed to raise rates at only a glacial pace. As I have been emphasizing, by narrowly defining excess, Fed policy makers ignored the growing housing bubble with its clear potential to wreak havoc somewhere down the road. As a consequence, the Fed started tightening too late, and it tightened much too slowly.

But the boom in housing benefited from more than a timid Fed. As the chart in Figure 10.4 reveals, for over a year, Fed-engineered increases in short-term interest rates had nearly no effect on the level

Figure 10.4

Greenspan's Conundrum: The Fed Lifts the Funds Rate, but Long-Term Interest Rates Completely Ignore the Rise

30-Year Jumbo Mortgage Rates vs. Federal Funds Target Rate

of long-term interest rates—including and especially fixed rate mortgages. In May 2004, on the eve of the Fed's first tightening move, conventional fixed rate mortgages were available at 5.9 percent. In December 2005, after the Fed raised short-term rates by over 3 percentage points, fixed rate mortgages were still available at 6.3 percent! Greenspan was bemused by the failure of long rates to rise. He went so far as to name the phenomenon. He called it a "conundrum."

It certainly was puzzling to me. I spent 2004 and 2005 incorrectly predicting that stepwise Fed tightening would lift long-term interest rates and temper the housing boom. Instead, steady increases in the Fed funds rate failed to tighten credit availability, and the housing boom built momentum.

Greenspan's soon-to-be successor, Ben Bernanke, offered up an explanation for the conundrum. A global savings glut, largely building up in Asia, was lowering real borrowing costs for investment projects in developed world economies. In other words, free-flowing international capital markets were lowering U.S. homeowner borrowing costs, because investment opportunities in Asian nations were limited.

Other observers, including me, came to believe a different story. China and a handful of other Asian countries were intent on keeping their currencies pegged to the U.S. dollar. To do so, they needed to buy U.S. bonds. And they ended up buying trillions of dollars' worth of U.S. Treasury bonds and mortgage backed bonds. In effect, Asian central banks were thwarting the Fed's effort to raise rates. As I put it, in a research report in 2006:

Who Is in Charge of U.S. Monetary Policy, Hu Indeed![2]

So Greenspan called it a conundrum. Bernanke explained it in terms of global savings. I saw it as easy money emanating from the

Asian central banks. Any way you sliced it, however, U.S. long-term interest rates were not responding to Fed policy actions. Thus, just as the late 1990s U.S. boom was in part a reaction to the Asian bust, the 2004-2005 housing boom in part reflected the rest of the world's influence on U.S. interest rates.

Does this absolve Greenspan/Bernanke from responsibility? No. The Fed was making two mistakes in the mid-2000s. It failed to focus on the housing bubble. And it ignored the absence of any tightening of credit in 2004-2005, comfortable in the knowledge that inflation was low and it was raising its target rate.

Fed miscalculation alongside Asian money flows kept U.S. mortgage rates low throughout much of the 1998-2005 period. And the extended good times for people in businesses tied to housing or housing finance created false confidences, financial innovations, euphoria, and ultimately fraud. In short, we witnessed the creation of a spectacular asset bubble.

The Key to the Kingdom: House Prices Never Fall!

As we saw with the strategy employed by Hanna in Chapter 3, buying a McMansion with next to no money down and with a small monthly paycheck can succeed—if the value of the property rises. Companies in the business of providing mortgage money to buyers like Hanna embraced the same basic model, as they created easier and easier ways for potential home buyers to get credit.

Why would any lenders, in their right minds, give money to buyers who put no money down and provided no paperwork on their monthly incomes? The lenders calculated that the losses from default would be limited, since they would end up owning the houses. Since house prices *always* go up, the mortgage holders would receive assets whose values were in excess of the monies loaned. Deadbeat borrowers notwithstanding, there really was no problem. True enough, the national median home price never fell from 1966 through 2002. And powerful mathematical models inputted that "truth."

The fact that many mortgage companies that issued credit to home buyers were not in the business of holding the mortgages created moral hazard. The mortgage originators collected fees and passed the mortgages to Wall Street firms. Wall Street sliced and diced mortgages and placed mortgage products—collateralized mortgage obligations—into the hands of institutional investors in the United States and around the world. Rating agencies, mesmerized by the math and oblivious to the need for ever higher home prices, gave triple A ratings to highly dubious mortgages. From afar, it was easy to buy the product with no real understanding of what you had.

Low Market Interest Rates + Creative Finance = Surging Home Prices

Wall Street convinced itself that mortgage products were safe because home prices did not fall. Home buyers, employing the same logic, embraced risky financing strategies in order to buy more house than they otherwise could. Hanna's approach to mortgage finance was taking hold.

For nearly five years this mutual admiration society between borrowers and lenders fed on itself. More to the point, it created a positive feedback loop. The bank is aggressively looking to lend money, thereby increasing the number of potential home buyers. This increase in demand drives home prices higher. Higher home prices make it easy for recent home buyers to refinance and take out extra cash to cover their mortgage payments. Foreclosures, as a consequence, remain very low. Mortgage providers point to low default levels as confirmation that their models are on track. Mortgage rocket scientists invent products with even easier initial terms. This further expands the pool of available home buyers. Home price gains accelerate. And the upward spiral is renewed.

From mid-2001 through mid-2005 this positive feedback loop took home prices to extraordinary levels. Most significant, the climb for home prices wildly outstripped income gains, climbing by nearly 10 percent per year, on average, in a time when incomes were growing at 4 percent per year. As the chart in Figure 10.5 shows, from mid-2001 through mid-2005 the median home price in the United States went from a bit less than 6 times the average person's available income

Figure 10.5

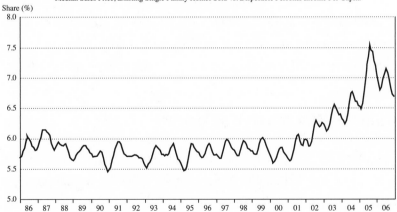

The Climb for House Prices
Outstripped Income Gains
Median Sales Price, Existing Single Family Homes Sold vs. Disposable Personal Income Per Capita

to nearly 8 times the income. In California, by early 2005, home prices were 11 times per capita income. Hanna's risky approach to mortgage finance was the only option new home buyers in California could employ. More to the point, betting that the home price would rise was the only way a buyer could make the mortgage payments over a multiyear period.

Surging home prices for existing homeowners, of course, was a bonanza. Real estate, due to home ownership, remains by far the biggest asset for most Americans. Rising home prices, therefore, translated into rising wealth for a great many people. And numerous studies revealed that in the 2001-2005 period, hundreds of billions of dollars of that wealth was being tapped into.

In the early 1990s we witnessed a multiyear refinancing boom that supported strong consumer spending. Homeowners turned in their 10 percent mortgages for 7 percent mortgages. This freed up cash for current purchases, given the new lower payments that were put into place. The refinancing boom of 2002-2005 was different. Interest rates were relatively steady. Homeowners improved their short-term purchasing power by increasing the size of their loans. They simply used the cash to finance current purchases. The result was a period in which consumer spending stayed strong despite the fact that rising energy and food prices were squeezing household purchasing power. Tapping into newfound housing wealth made homes into ATMs.

China as the Master of Vendor Finance?

Low mortgage rates, booming housing refinance, and strong consumer spending defined 2002-2005. Much of the spending was on products made in China. Incredibly, over the first five years of the new decade,

China's exports to the United States rose from 4 to 11 percent of nonauto U.S. retail spending. China's excitement about this export boom led directly to its strategy for conducting monetary policy. Central bank authorities were willing buyers of the U.S. dollar in order to make sure that there was very little change in the dollar/Chinese yuan exchange rate.

Accordingly, they bought the U.S. dollars that Chinese manufacturers collected for their exports. They bought the dollars that U.S. multinational corporations spent as they built factories in China. They bought the dollars U.S. investors funneled into Chinese real estate. In total, these purchases led to China's accumulating trillions of dollars' worth of U.S. Treasuries in a remarkably short period. If we accept the assertion that China's bond buying kept mortgage rates low in the United States, we come to an interesting conclusion. China kept U.S. long rates low by lending trillions to the United States. Low mortgage rates allowed Americans to borrow against their homes and use the proceeds to spend. And, increasingly, they bought products that were made in China—vendor financing on a trillion-dollar scale!

Emerging Nations Provide Low Interest Rates to the Developed World

It is instructive to focus on China, America, and housing when thinking about the bubble of 2002-2005. But if we look at asset markets and economies in the rest of the world, it's clear that similar dynamics were unfolding. Certainly, China's exports to Europe soared over the period. In fact, by late 2006, China exported as much to the European Union as it did to the United States. China also bought hundreds of billions of euros' worth of Continental sovereign bonds. Other emerging nations, including Russia, India, and Brazil, were giant buyers of developed world bonds, contributing to the low long-term interest rate backdrop that was in place.

An IMF study in 2006 showed that house prices were "well above fundamental values" in a long list of countries. Ireland, Britain, Australia, Norway, France, Sweden, and Spain all had serious house price inflation excesses. The simple truth was that interest rates were very easy in much of the developed world. And a housing bubble formed here, there, and almost everywhere.

The Overarching Euphoria: A Crazy Low Price for Risk

As the global economy improved in 2004-2005, central bankers in the United States and in much of the rest of the developed world began to raise interest rates. As I noted, these efforts were in part thwarted by enormous bond buying by emerging-economy central banks. We can see that in the nearly nonexistent rise for long-dated U.S. Treasury borrowing rates. More important, however, corporations actually saw their borrowing costs fall from late 2003 through late 2005, notwithstanding the Fed's increase of over 3 percentage points for its target overnight rate. As the chart in Figure 10.6 reveals, risky company borrowing costs were falling despite Fed tightening.

To put this in perspective, amidst the carnage of the technology bust, in 2002, a risky company—a Baa borrower—had to pay 5.5 percent, adjusted for inflation, to borrow. At that time, the federal government's real borrowing cost was 2.5 percent. The difference, of course, compensates the lender for the possibility that the company might go bankrupt. By late 2005 the same company's real borrowing

Figure 10.6

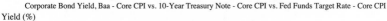

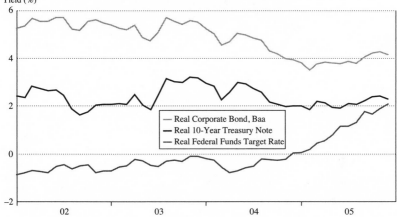

**Real Borrowing Rates for Risky Companies Fell and
Real Government Bond Yields Held Steady,
as the Real Fed Funds Rate Slowly Rose**

Corporate Bond Yield, Baa - Core CPI vs. 10-Year Treasury Note - Core CPI vs. Fed Funds Target Rate - Core CPI

Legend:
- Real Corporate Bond, Baa
- Real 10-Year Treasury Note
- Real Federal Funds Target Rate

rate had fallen to 4.25 percent despite the fact that the federal government was still being charged 2.5 percent. Most important, the fact that the Fed funds rate had been lifted over the period was irrelevant to borrowers in business. Their borrowing costs were lower, and the global boom was proof positive that they knew full well that it was so.

In summation, in 2005, despite a boom in housing and the reality of super low borrowing rates offered up to risky companies, the Fed and other developed-economy central banks were comfortable with the backdrop. Ultimately, rising energy prices pushed interest rates up. The ensuing bust first gripped the United States and then became a world recession. The dynamics that precipitated the U.S. recession, the global capital markets crisis, and the worldwide downturn, are the subject of the next two chapters.

Chapter | 11

BERNANKE'S CALAMITY AND THE ONSET OF U.S. RECESSION

If . . . we are tempted to assert that money is the drink which
stimulates the system to activity, we must remind ourselves that
there may be several slips between the cup and the lip.
—John Maynard Keynes, *The General Theory of Employment,*
Interest, and Money, 1936

How did boom become gloom? Risky finance in U.S. real estate and easy money in general came to an end, a consequence of capital market and central bank responses to surging energy and food prices. The last leg up for short-term interest rates and some belated rise for long-term interest rates finally weighed on the U.S. housing boom. Once the housing surge began to falter, the explosive positive feedback loop of 2002-2005 began to work in reverse.

When Fed ease proved as ineffectual as Fed tightening, it became apparent to those who understood the housing dynamic that a hard landing for housing could not be avoided. This was sure to weigh heavily on consumer spending and therefore spelled outright recession for the U.S. economy. The full implications of the hard fall for housing played out in the collapse of the existing financial economic order—following a dominolike fall of financial institutions.

Global market mayhem and consequent worldwide recession are the subjects of the chapter that follows this one.

The Crisis Begins in 2006, as Rising Mortgage Rates Pop the Housing Bubble

For conventional analysts, falling home prices in 2006 and early 2007 were a sideshow. Booming Asian economies had driven oil and other raw materials prices sharply higher, lifting worldwide inflation readings. In the United States, Fed interest rate increases, as of late 2005, were being matched by increases in long-term interest rates. Ten-year Treasury yields, locked in a tight range centered around 4.25 percent for several years, jumped and were yielding 5.25 percent by the spring of 2006. The fear among central bankers and in global bond markets was that unrelenting energy and food price increases might carry the day and stoke a generalized surge for global inflation.

Suddenly, the seemingly endless period of easy money to finance home purchases was coming under pressure. From late 2005 through mid-2006, fixed rate mortgages rose by a full percentage point. The 6 percent fixed rate was now a 7 percent fixed rate. Moreover, the cumulative rise for the Fed funds rate stood at over 4 percentage points by mid-2006. Thus, the initial interest rate charged for an adjustable rate mortgage was up sharply. The final climb for overnight rates had forced even the most creative mortgage providers to lift their teaser rates—the cost of money forced them to make the adjustment.

Starting in late 2005, home sales began to slow from what had been an unprecedented pace in 2004-2005. The falloff in demand for housing gave remaining home buyers some welcome advantage as they dickered over price. The results were not really surprising. House prices—after an unprecedented run and amidst faltering demand—began to fall. But we learned in Chapter 3 that by late 2005 around half of the newly issued mortgages were designed with Hanna's view of the world in mind. More to the point, rocket scientist models estimating the value of complex mortgage products were, in the end, just as susceptible to crisis as Hanna was if home prices started retreating. And by mid-2006 they were doing just that.

Rising house prices, Hanna taught us, allowed the subprime borrower to earn a capital gain on her house and miraculously be transformed into a prime borrower. Once house prices stopped rising, the mortgage market faced an immediate problem. At first it was confined to subprime borrowers and their lenders. But the dynamic of falling house prices quickly infected the entire housing industry.

Initially, the defaults were all in risky mortgages. But the wave of foreclosures that resulted precipitated acceleration on the downside for house prices. Soon enough it became apparent that no one was safe. Lower prices apply not just to houses financed with subprime mortgages, but to all houses. As a result, all mortgages backed by houses in areas where prices were falling began to lose value, even those made to prime borrowers. Wall Street firms found themselves knee deep in mortgages of questionable value. They were also the providers of credit to regional firms who were even deeper into mortgages.

In August 2007 the first panic ensued, and the housing crisis commanded everyone's attention. A majority of analysts began to recognize that home prices were destined to fall dramatically. The banks holding mortgage products had to radically reduce the values of these products on their balance sheets. The first in a succession of crises about the state of mortgage banking led to a wholesale change in attitudes about risk taking. Stocks fell sharply. Newfound anxieties about the bankruptcy risks jumped, and company borrowing rates soared. Not surprisingly, confidence in mortgage products imploded. Mortgage interest rates jumped to new highs for the cycle, as former buyers of mortgages backed away. For those who knew where to look, it was clear that the era of crazy easy finance was now in sharp retreat.

The Crisis Worsens as Central Banks Mistakenly Fight Inflation

Nonetheless, the U.S. Federal Reserve Board, still with a misguided fascination with headline price statistics, fought desperately to avoid lowering interest rates. As late as August 7, 2007, it contended that inflation was the primary risk that threatened the U.S. economy. Having failed to recognize the wild excesses in finance that dominated the landscape in 2005 and 2006, it symmetrically failed to appreciate the wild credit tightening taking place in 2007.

Mainstream commentary loudly echoed the Fed's focus on inflation. In August 2007, I was asked on CNBC to comment about prospective Fed policy. I volunteered that I thought that by the end of the year the funds rate would fall to 4 percent. Quite a few e-mails greeted me after the show, most of them critical, and one accused me of excessive use of hallucinogenic drugs. To give the consensus its due, the Fed tried to avoid lowering rates, again with a misguided focus on inflation. Nonetheless, the Fed funds rate ended the year at 4.25 percent, down from 5.25 percent—and it was lowered to 3 percent before the end of January 2008.

Figure 11.1

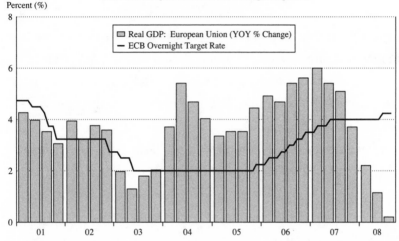

**Trichet Fiddled, While
Rome and Paris Burned**
Real GDP: European Union vs. ECB Overnight Target Rate

The European Central Bank, throughout 2007 and much of 2008, refused to ease. It actually tightened in July 2008 (see Figure 11.1). The ECB prides itself on its singular focus on wage and price pressures. When it held rates firm in early September, officials actually took a bow for their July tightening and explained that they were keenly interested in the wage settlement with the German union IG Metall, due to be struck that month. Thus, within days of the biggest financial crisis since the 1930s, ECB officials were worried about a particular union's wage settlement.

What happens if the 2009 recession is brutal? European leaders would be right to recommend that the ECB be considered for the Andrew Mellon Policy Blunder of the Century Award. Mellon, in charge of the U.S. Federal Reserve in the 1930s, actually tightened interest rates in the early years of the Great Depression. He too was convinced at the time that he was doing the right thing.

In the United States, a vocal group of economists supported the ECB. Once again, misguided confidence in the cleansing nature of bankruptcies *anywhere* led them to argue that failing financial institutions were *a sign that the system is working.* This led to the wildly incorrect assertion that aggressive Fed ease, in contrast to steadfast tight money in Europe, proved that the United States would soon face a major rise in inflation. Inflation nutcases had a final few months of glory as the U.S. dollar fell and oil and other commodity prices locked in one last crazy surge.

I have no qualms about labeling the last leg up for commodity prices "crazy." All of postwar history tells us that when global economies falter, commodity prices fall. Nonetheless, in the first half of 2008, sinking U.S. and European economic momentum was ignored. China alone, the argument went, would somehow keep commodities rising. Never mind that 10 minutes of research on the Chinese economy would reveal that it was an export machine completely dependent on U.S. and European consumer spending! When the commodity bubble burst, the reversal was breathtaking. The six-month slide for raw industrial prices broke a postwar record. And the decline for oil prices set a record as well.

Greenspan's Conundrum Becomes Bernanke's Calamity

To his credit, Ben Bernanke was well ahead of his European Central Bank colleagues. He recognized the need to reverse course and ease aggressively. But he soon confronted a frightening reality. Fed ease was met with rising mortgage rates. Greenspan's conundrum had become Bernanke's calamity.[1]

Why were climbing mortgage rates a calamity? Simply put, because they derailed the most painless way out of the mushrooming U.S. housing crisis. Frederick Mishkin, a Federal Reserve Board governor, laid out the arithmetic in compelling fashion.[2] He explained that potential home buyers had to think about two things when evaluating a home purchase. The first was the mortgage rate. The second was their sense of what future home prices would do. If mortgage rates are 6 percent and you believe the house price will rise by 4 percent, you face a 2 percent cost to acquire the capital to buy a home. During the boom, people were confident that house prices would continue to rise rapidly, so they were confident that the cost to secure capital to buy a home was extremely low. When housing prices reversed, in 2006, it became clear that expectations had been excessively optimistic. Mishkin pointed out that the key to rescuing housing was to short-circuit growing pessimism about home prices.

How might the Fed stop deteriorating confidence about home prices? Remember that Mishkin said two financial variables were juggled in home buyers' brains. House price expectations *and mortgage rates* combined to determine a home buyer's cost of capital. Accordingly, if the Fed could drive mortgage rates lower, it could lower home buyers' sense of the capital cost to buy a home. In so doing it would improve demand for homes. Rising demand for homes could well stem the slide for current house prices and thereby alleviate fears of house price declines in the years to come.

But the Fed was unable to implement the Mishkin strategy. From the fall of 2007 through mid-2008 the Fed lowered its target interest rate to 2 percent from 5.25 percent. But mortgage rates rose. Rising borrowing rates for households, in the midst of aggressive Fed ease,

Figure 11.2

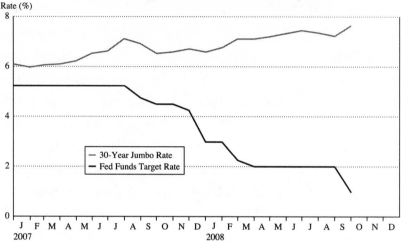

**Bernanke's Calamity: The Fed Lowers
the Funds Rate but Mortgage Rates Rise!**

U.S. Home Mortgage 30-Year Jumbo vs. Federal Funds Target Rate

ended any hope of a simple short-circuiting of the adverse feedback loop that gripped the housing market (see Figure 11.2).

Why did mortgage rates rise during the aggressive Fed ease? Initial mainstream commentary tied the rising mortgage rates to fears of future inflation and the weakness of the U.S. dollar, brought about when the Fed eased and the ECB stood firm. But that explanation died in mid-2008. At that time, confidence in the ECB evaporated, and the European currency plunged. And commodity prices began their free fall. How could mortgage rates rise amidst a soaring dollar and disappearing worries about inflation?

Simple. The rise reflected the wholesale collapse of confidence in the entire mortgage finance industry. As Bernanke, a master of understatement, put it in late October 2008:

The financial crisis has upset the linkage between mortgage borrowers and capital markets and has revealed a number of important problems in our system of mortgage finance. . . .[3]

For Minsky, the phenomenon of rising long rates alongside falling short rates was hardly novel. And the dynamic, in short order, depressed the real economy. In a crisis, Minsky wrote:

All of the internally generated funds are utilized to repay debt. A major objective of business, bankers, and financial intermediaries in this situation is to clean up their balance sheets. [This] can tend to sustain, and may even raise long-term interest rates even as short-term interest rates are decreasing.

We are no longer in a boom; we are in a debt deflation process [as] a feedback from the purely financial developments . . . [to the real economy] . . . takes place.[4]

The mad dash to reduce risk exposure, the dominolike falls of financial service companies, and the morphing of the U.S. recession into a global capital markets crisis and a worldwide recession are the subject of the next chapter.

Chapter | 12

DOMINO DEFAULTS, GLOBAL MARKETS CRISIS, AND END OF THE GREAT MODERATION

You're nothing but a pack of cards.
—Lewis Carroll, *Alice's Adventures in Wonderland*, 1865

We are all connected—most especially at Minsky moments. The chain of events that took the world from a spate of U.S. subprime lending defaults to a global capital markets crisis will be the subject of many books. What follows here is my bare description of the essential elements.

Once subprime borrower defaults began to drive home prices lower, the jig was up on the world's greatest Ponzi scheme, and it was only a matter of time until financial service companies of all kinds came under pressure. Combine a major episode of failed Ponzi finance with a moment's worth of misguided enthusiasm for Schumpeter's creative destruction, and you have a recipe for global capital markets mayhem. We witnessed both in 2008, and the biggest financial markets crisis since the 1930s took hold as the year came to a close.

As I noted in the last chapter, rapidly falling home prices started the destruction by blowing up all the estimates of the value of previously issued mortgages. Wall Street firms in the business of slicing and dicing mortgages were knee deep in questionable mortgage products. Not surprisingly, this deterioration caused their stock prices to plunge and their borrowing costs to jump. No one was panicking, but that was because they did not see what lay ahead.

Mortgage availability also tightened as the ultimate holders of mortgage products began to get queasy about extending home buyers any more credit. Banks, insurance companies, mutual funds, hedge funds, and even government-backed mortgage agencies stepped back. New home buyers soon discovered it was getting harder to qualify for a mortgage. By the middle of 2007, subprime lending had just about stopped, but prime borrowers could qualify for mortgages of less than a million. By the spring of 2008, the only buyers who qualified were those who didn't really need a mortgage, and even they had to pay a higher rate.

It doesn't require much training in finance to see that the elements of a housing disaster were in place. Supply was rising because houses that had previously been started were hitting the market alongside bank sales of foreclosed homes. Demand was falling as a consequence of tightening mortgage availability and higher borrowing costs. With increasing supply and declining demand, prices can only fall. And they did. Given the inflated level of house prices, it wouldn't have taken much to get prices moving downward, and this was more than not much. By spring 2008 house price declines of a magnitude Wall Street rocket scientists had dismissed as impossible became the reality. Falling values caused whatever prospective buyers who still remained to back away, so prices fell faster. Meanwhile, the value of paper secured by mortgages collapsed, and within a year securities that had a face value upon issuance of nearly $2 trillion had a market value closer to $1 trillion, if there was any market at all.

A brutal housing recession took hold and soon spread. U.S. consumers discovered that their access to easy cash through mortgages and home equity loans was gone. They stopped spending, and as 2007 came to a close, the country entered recession.

Lehman's Fall, Panic in Corporate Bonds, and a Global Capital Markets Crisis

The arrival of recession, a consequence of a burst bubble that fostered investment excesses, described every U.S. downturn since the mid-1980s. Failed financial institutions are always a part of the crisis in Minsky's framework. But the 2008-2009 downturn was different. For the first time since the 1930s, the creditworthiness of the world's banking system—not just individual banks—was called into question. Ordinary business in the world of finance depends upon the shared belief that parties to any transaction will hold up their end of any bargain. "I'm good for the money" is an implicit notion in day-to-day dealings. Once you lose confidence in the soundness of the people on the other side of the table, financial business comes to a screeching halt, and the global economy is not far behind.

Bear Stearns

Appropriately enough, the first firm to fail was Bear Stearns, the then-reigning world champion at slicing and dicing mortgages. Bear had for years earned fortunes by gathering mortgages from shaky borrowers and mixing them into cocktails, a remarkable number of which came out with triple A ratings. By the spring of 2008 it became clear that Bear just had too much mortgage paper on its own balance sheet, and with values falling daily, the firm simply ran out of capital. Other firms refused to do business with it, and the Federal Reserve and the Treasury then stepped in and arranged a merger with JPMorgan Chase.

The Treasury/Federal Reserve strategy in dealing with the Bear Stearns insolvency was consistent with Minsky's sense of the cost of capitalism. As this book makes clear, periodic financial market mayhem comes with the territory in a capitalist system. It is government's role to prevent systemic failure, and in so doing, to prevent the reappearance of an economic depression. Governments need to understand the difference between creative destruction and deflationary destruction. Looked upon in that light, the Bear Stearns deal was intelligently designed.

The terms of the agreement seemed to represent a good balance between the need to protect the system and the need to punish the excessive risk takers. The stockholders in Bear Stearns were more or less wiped out.[1] All employee contracts were abrogated, and employees were laid off en masse. No bonuses were paid, and many employees who had received prior bonuses in the form of company stock watched many years of back pay all but disappear. No one watching the collapse at Bear Stearns missed the point. Bear had miscalculated and it was paying the ultimate price.

Nonetheless, Bear did not declare bankruptcy. Thus, the company's creditors—the firms and clients to whom Bear owed money—were protected. And by protecting the thousands of credit links that Bear had with the rest of the financial system, the Treasury/Federal Reserve plan wiped Bear off the map and yet minimized the adverse consequences to the system.

Lehman Brothers

After Bear's demise, financial markets stabilized for a short while. Recessionary forces dissipated for a bit, as tax rebates gave some small bounce to consumer spending. The seed of doubt, however, had been planted. If mortgage losses could bring down Bear Stearns, weren't there other firms equally vulnerable? Indeed there were, and attention soon focused upon Lehman Brothers. In the mortgage market, Lehman had comparable exposure to mortgage finance, though the firm in its entirety was more diverse. Nevertheless, the same questions about solvency that undid Bear eventually got to Lehman, and the firm faced its own crisis.

In this case, however, the Treasury and the Federal Reserve stood aside. Lehman Brothers exhausted all other options and declared bankruptcy on September 15, 2008. This meant that investors in Lehman's commercial paper and corporate bonds were essentially wiped out. And in an instant a global bank run was under way.

When Lehman declared bankruptcy, I was shocked.[2] I had been convinced that government officials understood the gravity of the situation they faced. I had in fact counseled clients that they could depend upon the Bear Stearns precedent. If you owned stock in a suspect financial institution, I ventured, you could lose everything if it failed to quickly turn things around. Thus, a forced merger for Lehman, with the stock price valued at next to nothing, seemed to be the clear fate it faced. But the Treasury and the Fed, I was convinced, recognized the severity of the crisis that would confront them if they permitted the bankruptcy of a major financial institution.

The Treasury justified its inaction by arguing that, unlike the Bear situation, Lehman's failure was not a sudden event, and investors and other banks had had enough time to insulate themselves from any damaging exposure to Lehman's debts. More philosophically, Bush administration officials let it be known that they wanted to demonstrate their zeal for the cleansing nature of markets. Lehman had failed. Anyone tied to its fortunes had to suffer the consequences. It was misguided faith in free markets and a wildly off-base celebration of Schumpeter's creative destruction. To me it was simply dumbfounding. Within 24 hours the world appreciated just how dumb it was.

Frozen Credit

By establishing the "Bear precedent," the government had lessened worries about lending risks. Once it let Lehman go, those worries exploded. The example of a financial institution of Lehman's size and standing being allowed to fail without compensation to even the holders of its short-term debts put the financial world into outright panic. The market for commercial paper, a $1 trillion market by which businesses finance inventories and working capital, all but closed. Commercial banks became unwilling to lend to one another, much less to their customers. Money market mutual funds suffered withdrawals of over $500 billion in a matter of days, and the yields on Treasury bills, the safest of safe havens, fell below zero!

The Treasury zeal for ideological purity did not survive the week. On Monday, Lehman was allowed to go bankrupt. On Tuesday, September 16, the Federal Reserve and the Treasury authorized the New York Fed to lend AIG $85 billion. Thus, their refusal to construct a workout for an investment bank, in short order, forced them to bail out an insurance company!

The episode's culminating event took place in early September when the General Electric Company, one of America's few remaining triple A enterprises, was forced to sell stock to raise cash because it was unable to raise money by issuing commercial paper. The market, even for G.E., was closed.

It didn't take long for the world to appreciate the macroeconomic significance of a frozen credit market. Without access to short-term credit, any number of companies that operated well outside the world of finance were placed in jeopardy. That was true of large well-established companies, but it hit new companies especially hard. Within weeks, the borrowing rates on high-yield corporate bonds rose by 5 percentage points or more. All of a sudden ordinary people all over the world learned the meaning of the letters CDO.

Collateralized Debt Obligations

Collateralized debt obligations are a market where companies buy and sell insurance on corporate bonds. Any CDO is a promise between a buyer and a writer of the insurance. If things go as planned, the buyer pays the insurer the premium. If things go awry, the insurer pays the buyer. Either way, one of the two parties gets the money promised in the transaction. That makes the CDO market, in theory, a zero sum game.

For the overall financial system, the argument went, there is no risk, because Harry's loss will always be Sally's gain. That logic prevailed, and the market grew without any serious regulatory oversight.

By mid-2007, the CDO market had the implausibly high value of $55 trillion. It amounted to a mountain of wagers about corporate bonds that dwarfed the value of the underlying securities themselves.

Where was the faulty logic that made this mountain a potentially crushing burden? What happens if Harry owes Sally and he cannot pay because he is bankrupt? What if Sally was depending on Harry's payment to keep her in good financial stead? She might be forced into bankruptcy and be unable to honor her CDO payments to Freddy. Suddenly, in the aftermath of the Lehman bankruptcy, a $55 trillion market appeared as another rocket science creation that had potential disaster written all over it. And bank bailouts littered the landscape over the weeks immediately ahead.

Trying to Squelch a Global Bank Run

Actions speak louder than words. The events of 2007-2008 leave no room for debate. There is simply no place for free market ideologues in a banking crisis. The Lehman bankruptcy put that notion to rest in a heartbeat. I don't want to overplay the importance of Lehman's treatment by government officials. It could well be that the system was simply too ripe for a riot, and the catalyst was incidental. But one thing is certain. Letting Lehman go on ideological grounds was a complete bust. Within weeks, Big Government actions were the rule around the globe. In less than two months the Bush administration did the following:

- Goldman Sachs was converted to a commercial bank from an investment bank.

- Washington Mutual was seized by federal regulators and melded into JPMorgan Chase.

- The Federal Reserve created the Commercial Paper Funding Facility.
- Congress approved a $700 billion rescue plan for the banking system.
- The Treasury forced leading U.S. banks to take a government infusion of capital.

U.S. actions occurred alongside major steps around the world:

- The U.K. Treasury made $350 billion available for recapitalizing U.K. banks.
- The Swiss National Bank provided capital to UBS.
- Sweden enacted a $250 billion package to stabilize its financial sector.

A global banking crisis, requiring broad, sweeping bailouts, and a deepening worldwide recession are the realities in place as this book goes to print. How large a price the world will pay for embracing the notion of market infallibility remains to be seen. But no one should doubt the fact that the world needs more than new leadership. We need a new paradigm, one that reflects how the world really works. In this book's final chapter I offer up some preliminary thoughts on the issue of policy, from a global perspective in a postcrisis world. In the chapter that follows, I sketch out the mainstream economic theory that informed policy makers in the years leading up to 2008-2009.

Part | **IV**

RECASTING ECONOMIC THEORY FOR THE TWENTY-FIRST CENTURY

Chapter | 13

ECONOMIC ORTHODOXY ON THE EVE OF THE CRISIS

[Classical] theorists have at their command an impressive array of proven techniques for modeling systems that 'always work well'. Keynesian economists have experience with modeling systems that 'never work'. But as yet no one has the recipe for modeling systems that function pretty well most of the time but sometimes work very badly to coordinate economic activities.

—Axel Leijonhufvud, "Schools, Revolutions, and Research Programmes in Economic Theory" in *Method and Appraisal in Economics*, edited by Spiro Latsis, Cambridge University Press, 1976

A critical assertion made in this book is that key policy errors were made that contributed to the 2008 crisis, and that these errors were strategic not tactical. By that I mean the game plan was wrong, not its day-to-day operations. Policy, as you would expect, was a product of today's conventional economic wisdom. And as such, mainstream economic theory, and its architects, must accept some of the blame for the upheaval that came to a climax in autumn 2008.

Fans of the book *Freakonomics* will find nothing unsettling about the criticisms that follow in this chapter. That fantastically popular economics book uses state-of-the-art microeconomic theory to shed light on some unusual topics. As the names suggest, micro theory trains its eyes on particular markets and sectors. Macroeconomics, in contrast, focuses on economywide issues. How an individual consumer might respond to a sharp rise in gasoline prices is the subject of micro theory. What consumers, taken together, might do, and what that would mean for the overall economy, is the subject of macro theory.[1] In this chapter we train our sights on the current state of macro theory.

Macroeconomic Fundamentals

There are two essential observations that can be made about economies. One: over long periods, growth is the rule. Two: with remarkable regularity, free market economies suffer from boom and bust cycles.

In simplest terms we can say that macroeconomists who embrace classical traditions celebrate the "invisible hand" that guides free markets and produces trajectories like the one depicted in Figure 13.1. Keynes and his followers concentrated their focus, wondering why economies, periodically, suffer from bouts of high joblessness, falling production, and widespread bankruptcies (see Figure 13.2). Paul Samuelson had this to say about Keynes:

> Keynes denies that there is an Invisible Hand channeling the self-centered action of each individual to the social optimum. This is the sum and substance of his heresy.[2]

Figure 13.1

**Growth Is the Goal
and Growth Is the Rule**
NIPA: Real GDP

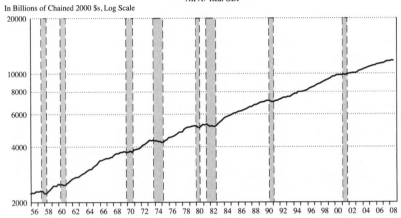

In Billions of Chained 2000 $s, Log Scale

Figure 13.2

**Dad's Dictum: "It's a Second Derivative World."
Changes in Growth Rates Animate Economic Opinion.**
NIPA: Real GDP

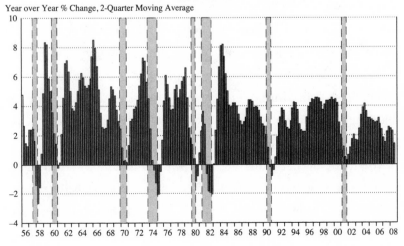

Year over Year % Change, 2-Quarter Moving Average

What prompted Keynes to break company with the classical economists of his day? The Great Depression devastated the global economy. In the United States, unemployment reached 25 percent, industrial production fell by 40 percent as stocks fell by 90 percent, and 9,600 banks failed. Everywhere he looked, economic reality was at odds with the notion of a self-correcting system. Keynes's revolutionary work, *The General Theory of Employment, Interest, and Money*, set in motion a debate that, sadly, seems as unresolved today as it was in 1936 when his groundbreaking effort made its first appearance.

Classical economists before Keynes argued that free markets process information flawlessly and lead economies to healthy places. Keynes disagreed, and his early admirers built models aimed at sketching out the role that government should play in tempering periods of falling activity and overall economic decline. As is true with all great works, debate raged even among the admirers of Keynes about what the general theory actually said.

Three groups emerged. Classical economists championed free market economic traditions and rejected Keynes's assertions about the inherent flaws of capitalism. Keynesians cobbled together an amalgam of insights from Keynes and classical beliefs, forging what became known as the "neoclassical synthesis." And Post-Keynesian economists, including Hyman Minsky, rejected the neoclassical synthesis, arguing that much of the genius of Keynes was lost in the attempt to preserve the lion's share of the classical economic tradition.

To grossly oversimplify, the groups fared as follows: Keynesians ruled the roost in the 1950s and 1960s. The 1970s was a battleground. Monetarists, the first group that refocused on classical traditions, had a brief heyday in the late seventies and early eighties. The classical economists of evolving stripes, despite their limited numbers, provided important support for conservative Washington ideologues in the 1980s and into the 1990s.

As we complete this decade, we are in a similar position to the mid-1970s. The reign of the free market fundamentalists is now clearly over. Traditional Keynesians, not surprisingly, are clamoring for their shot at the throne. Many Post-Keynesians see today's economic plight as an opportunity to push for radical change. But we need economists to do better than that.

As I have emphasized throughout this book, we need a new paradigm to emerge, one that accepts two self-evident truths:

1. Sensibly regulated free market capitalism does the best job of delivering growth to the citizenry of the world.

2. Financial system excesses are the root cause of many boom and bust cycles.

The previous 12 chapters, I believe, make it hard to argue with these two truths. But in the land of academic economics, embracing these notions will require some heavy lifting:

- Classical economists have to acknowledge that periods of economic decline reflect flaws in capitalism that justify the visible hand of government intervention.

- Both classical and Keynesian economists have to accept that these flaws arise in the world of finance, and that they reflect the uncertain and at times emotion-filled world we live in.

- And Post-Keynesians, giddy in the knowledge that they have cracked the code, need to come to terms with the fact that, flaws and all, free market capitalism is vastly superior to government-directed investment strategies.

The rest of this chapter will deal with the views of classical and mainstream Keynesian economists. The chapter that follows is devoted to Minsky and the post-Keynesians. I am the most critical of new classical economics, because in its final form it is close to nonsensical. But the New Keynesians need to amend their theories. For both groups, the persistence of certain economic realities can no longer be ignored.

From a Great Monetarist Victory to an Implausible Theory

Unfortunately for economic policy makers and for the world at large, economists after Keynes have fought the same fight in different guises, generation by generation. Once scientists established that the earth revolved around the sun, the Ptolemaic system was permanently made obsolete. No one stood up 50 years later with new research aimed at reestablishing that the sun revolved around the earth. Not so in macroeconomics. Belief in the infallibility of markets, by the mid-1980s, reemerged as real business cycle theory, only 50 years after the Great Depression.

How did economic theory wind its way back to belief in infallible markets? Unquestionably, Keynesians opened the door for a reemergence of classical economic thinking because they overpromised. In the early 1960s, Keynesians asserted that they had developed monetary and fiscal policy tools that would allow them to "fine-tune" the economy and eliminate the boom and bust cycle. By the mid-1970s, amidst soaring inflation and a deep recession, confidence in fine-tuning policies collapsed.

Economists who championed free market solutions correctly declared that Keynesians had overreached. Led by Milton Friedman, they asserted that monetary policy should be conducted with only one focus—controlling the flow of money into the economy. The boom and bust cycle, they argued, was tolerable. And attempts to eliminate it, given the limited information policy makers had, only led to higher inflation and deeper recessions down the road.[3] Friedman's assessment carried the day. In 1976 he was awarded the Nobel prize.

Rational expectations became the next cornerstone of conservative efforts. In simplest terms, the theory says that government attempts to steer the economy are doomed to failure, because people will see through the government policies. If the government enacts a spending program—for instance, to create jobs—people know that it will require big borrowing. They will sell bonds, correctly anticipating a surge in government bond issuance. If enough people sell bonds, the prices fall. And when prices fall, yields rise. So simply the fear of big budget deficits to come drives interest rates up, and the benefit of more jobs from the stimulus program is completely wiped out by the lost jobs that result from higher long-term rates. According to this line of thought, people are too smart to be fooled by these government efforts to improve the economy in the short run. They are rational, and as policies are put in place, they will change their expectations about the future and thereby thwart the government's plans.

The rational expectations conclusion? Better to keep government very small, keep the Fed focused on delivering low inflation, and let the markets and the private sector deliver the jobs and economic growth as best they can.

In 1979, President Jimmy Carter appointed Paul Volcker the new head of the U.S. Federal Reserve Board. Volcker adopted a strategy long championed by Friedman. He declared that he would ignore interest rate changes and conduct monetary policy by controlling growth in the money supply. Most important, because the Fed asserted that it was targeting money growth, it was able to claim that it was not directly responsible for rapidly rising interest rates. And because the Fed was committed to driving inflation lower, rational expectations enthusiasts argued that the fall in inflation would not necessarily require severe economic distress.

The policy worked, but not through any painless change in attitudes. Instead, inflation was driven lower by crushing economic activity. In the second quarter of 1980, real GDP fell at a whopping 7.8 percent annualized rate. More incredibly, real GDP, in the fourth quarter of 1982 was virtually at the same level as in the last quarter of 1978. Unemployment, at 5.8 percent when Volcker was installed as chairman, climbed to 10.8 percent by late 1982. Thus, the Volcker war against inflation had required back-to-back recessions and resulted in no growth over four full years! But it did the trick. Inflation fell sharply, from over 13 percent in 1979 to under 4 percent by early 1983. The battle had been won.[4]

Thus, conservative economic thinking delivered the world a great triumph. Nothing succeeds like success. And in academia, in Washington, and on Main Street, conservative economic thinking was on the rise.

From Invisible to Infallible Hand: New Classical Economics and Real Business Cycles

Friedman's victory over fine-tuning changed the way people thought about the U.S. Federal Reserve Board and about central banks around the world. Monetary policy was deemed to be responsible for keeping inflation low. Low inflation, in turn, was thought to offer a market-driven economy its best chance for healthy economic growth over the long haul.

The Reagan revolution complemented the monetary policy overhaul. Government programs, regulations, and taxes were slashed. It was a counterrevolution, effectively dismantling much of the government infrastructure that had been justified on Keynesian interventionist grounds.[5]

It was a simple message and it carried the day. Monetary policy would keep inflation low. Private initiative, stripped of government encumbrances, would propel the economy.

What about recessions, with the big rise for unemployment that is the earmark of a period of economic decline? Didn't Fed policy makers still need to be willing to come to the economy's rescue during a contraction? Keynesian theorists, although now on the defensive, remained adamant that a recession was Exhibit A for anyone needing evidence that, with some regularity, free markets fail to get us where we need to go.

Think for a moment about the labor market. Workers *supply* labor. Employers *demand* labor. The price of labor is how much people get paid. Wage rates shift, standard micro theory tells us, until the number of people who want to work at that wage level just equals the number of employers who will hire people at that wage rate. We then have that magical circumstance for economists, *equilibrium.*

If you study recessions, however, you start to get queasy about labor markets and equilibrium. What happens, quite regularly, is that wage rates don't fall. Instead, more and more people get fired, and unemployment climbs, in many cases for over a year.

As we will detail in the section that follows, the fact that wage rates don't fall during recessions remained a key piece of the New Keynesian framework. But conservative economists were hell-bent on championing free markets at any and all times.

Why such adamancy about the dangers of government intervention? The battle among policy makers was for very high stakes. Are there times when the government needs to take direct action to ensure that the economy gives as much to its citizens as it can? Can we justify building roads and bridges on the basis of the fact that people need jobs and the economy isn't providing them? Can we tell the Fed to stimulate the economy by lowering interest rates and printing more money, because we view a period of high unemployment as unacceptable?

Over the early postwar years, the answer to all of these questions was always a resounding YES. The Great Depression haunted the World War II generation, and government policy makers, when confronting a weak economy, had Keynesian theory and the backing of the majority as they consistently intervened. Tax cuts, spending increases, and big ease from the Fed all were employed, to substantial excess, when the economy disappointed.

But the legacy of freewheeling government meddling, with Keynesian justification, was the Great Inflation of the 1960s and 1970s. The descendants of Milton Friedman had a victory in hand. And they were desperate for a rationale that would allow them to assert that at all times the visible hand of government help was a bad idea.

Dr. Pangloss Discovers Real Business Cycles

Monetary policy debates between Keynesians and classical economists can be reduced to discussions of rules versus discretion. Economists of classical descent want central banks to follow an unwavering script. Monetary policy makers, when they have wiggle room, make matters worse. Friedman argued, correctly, that the government had too little information about the economy to fine-tune it. His admonition to target money supply growth turned out to be inoperable in practice. Taken as metaphor for a rejection of fine-tuning, however, its appeal endured.

The rational expectations school effectively said that disappointing circumstances, like a recession, might be lamentable, but government efforts couldn't help.[6] This still left the door ajar for policy makers to defend intervention strategies. After all, the theory did not say that things are always optimal; it just claimed you were unlikely to make them better. What was needed was a framework that justified any and all economic circumstances as the best that you could have at that time.

In academia, at around the same time, economists decided that macroeconomic theories were not legitimate unless they were built from the bottom up. The idea was to think of a single well-informed and rational person or company, investigate how that person or company would operate, and expand this foundation so it explained the overall economy but remained true to these microeconomic underpinnings.

For conservatives, a home run theory from an analytic and policy perspective would cover both bases. It would have bottom-up foundations. And it would conclude that markets are infallible.

Enter real business cycles.[7] In this world, the ups and downs of the economy reflect changes in the rate at which we invent things. To real business cycle theorists, classical explanations for long-term growth and Schumpeter's idea's about creative destruction explain both the long run *and the short run.* Thus, from the perspective of conservative policy makers, the job was now done. Whatever the economic situation, it was the best of all possible worlds.

The problem with real business cycle theory is that it is nonsense, pure and simple. Readers who know that new classical theorists collected five Nobel prizes may be worried that my scorn says more about my need for psychological counseling than it does about the problems with real business cycle theories. I could defend my assertion by pointing to the long list of those in opposition to new classical economists who have won Nobel prizes over the past 20 years. But there is a much better defense.

In plain English I will highlight four key real business cycle conclusions, then ask readers to cast their votes. Who is crazy, me or them?

1. If your boss surprises you with a $5,000 bonus, you won't change your spending plans, given your focus on your long-run income path.

2. When the unemployment rate soars, during recessions, it is not because people can't find work but because the weak economy now offers lower wages and workers decide *voluntarily* that it's a good time to take a year off and enjoy an extended vacation.

3. When people en masse were buying dot-com stocks with no earnings and in some cases no business plans, on borrowed money, it reflected rational judgments by thoughtful investors.

4. Last, and my favorite: No matter how much the U.S. Federal Reserve Board raises or lowers interest rates, it cannot affect the real economy. Fed decisions to move interest rates may drive inflation higher or lower, but the real economy cannot be influenced by monetary policy moves.[8]

Maybe I'm not so crazy? Indeed, the four conclusions that I detail above are outrageous. Ask people in a bar how they'd respond if their employers handed them bonuses, and they'll tick off their spending wish lists. Ask an unemployed guy in a bar if he is enjoying his extended vacation and you may well have asked your last question. Joseph E. Stiglitz, a renegade Keynesian who collected his own Nobel prize, put it this way:

> The attempts made to construct a new macroeconomics based on traditional microeconomics, with its assumptions of well-functioning markets, was doomed to failure. Recessions and depressions, accompanied by massive unemployment, were symptomatic of massive market failures. The market for labor was clearly not clearing. How could a theory that began with the assumption that all markets clear ever provide an explanation?[9]

As it turns out, many great minds in pursuit of a theory that unified micro- and macroeconomics lost their way. Even today some defend these efforts, claiming that their failure to square with economic reality, to date, is only temporary.

That is a perfectly reasonable defense for an abstract physicist. Washington Taylor of MIT fame uses it on his Web site:

> String theory is currently the most promising candidate for a unified theory for Physics. It is still not possible, however, to define string theory in a space-time background compatible with the physics we see around us, and string theory cannot yet be used to make predictions.[10]

But Professor Taylor's efforts to reconcile electromagnetic forces with the forces of gravity have not ruffled real-world feathers. Electricians remain confident in their abilities to wire your house, and plumbers are cocksure that sewage flows downhill.

Unfortunately, policy makers were clearly influenced by the latest generation of economists of the classical school. Indeed, I would submit that Fed policy makers, Treasury officials, and other key players over the past two dozen years made bad decisions in part because they let themselves believe that sewage really could, on occasion, flow uphill.

New Keynesians Drink Half a Glass of Kool-Aid

Keynesians of any stripe, by definition, accept the notion that market failures are possible. New Keynesians took the bait, however, when criticized by their new classical competition, and set out to establish microeconomic foundations for Keynesian conclusions. And to do that, the math required them to embrace the notion that people in general act rationally.

Boom and bust cycles are not ideal, according to New Keynesians. But they agree with their new classical colleagues that there is no long-run inflation/unemployment trade-off. The key market imperfection that drives cycles is found in the labor market. Wages are sticky. An unlucky group loses their jobs because the majority keeps their wage rates intact.

This leads New Keynesians halfway toward the new classical formulation in their design of monetary policy:

- They agree that keeping inflation low is the main job for the central bank.
- They agree that there is no long-run inflation/unemployment trade-off.

- They train their sights on the real economy and inflation, giving Wall Street sideshow status.

The Taylor rule best captures their efforts. The equation directs the monetary authorities to adjust nominal interest rates in reaction to inflation and output. If output is below potential amidst low inflation, the central bank delivers low interest rates. When inflation rises above target, the central bank raises rates, confident that the temporary high unemployment period that ensues will lower inflation.

What is the key difference between New Keynesian and new classical directives toward the central bank? New classical economists argue that the sole job for the central bank is to keep inflation low. A big jump for joblessness, in their world, should be ignored as long as stable prices are in view. New Keynesian economists direct the central bank to lower rates and stimulate if the economy has clearly hit a bad patch.

The New Keynesian formulation sees demand and supply shocks as the destabilizing forces, but like new classical theorists, they judge wage and price inflation as the key symptom of imbalance. They embrace the notion that markets are rational. Therefore, if inflation is stable, excesses are absent, and Fed policy makers can relax.

In general, that is what central bankers have done over the past 25 years. Focusing on wages and prices, they saw no excesses. When confronted with breathtaking market advances, they quoted efficient markets rhetoric. And the financial system bust of 2008 and the global 2008-2009 recession are the price the world is now paying.

Post-Keynesians, especially acolytes of Hyman Minsky, watched the developments leading up to the 2008 crisis with morbid fascination. An impressive number of papers were published from 2004 through

2006 that warned of the extraordinary risks building in the world's financial system.

If Minsky and his followers had a central Keynesian foundation, it was their focus on the speculative nature of long-term expectations. As Keynes put it:

> . . . the orthodox theory assumes that we have a knowledge of the future of a kind quite different from that which we actually possess.[11]

In the next chapter I will argue that for modern day economists, Keynes without Minsky is something like Caesar without the Bard.

Chapter | 14

MINSKY AND MONETARY POLICY

*Pollyanna was much happier than Cassandra. But the Cassandric
components of our nature are necessary for survival. . . . The benefit
of foreseeing catastrophe is the ability to take steps to avoid it,
sacrificing short-term for long-term benefits.*
—Carl Sagan, *The Dragons of Eden,* 1986

In the mid-1970s, as the worst recession since the Great Depression
was ending, Hyman Minsky published a book championing the
insights of J. M. Keynes. It was a bizarre moment to offer up this analysis. Keynesian economic theories were under siege. Milton Friedman,
the poster child for free market capitalism, would soon collect his
Nobel prize. In addition, over the next 20 years economists in the
classical tradition would reclaim center stage in both academia and
Washington. Minsky, unruffled, offered the world the monograph
John Maynard Keynes in the fall of 1975.

For Minsky, the deep economic troubles that confronted the United
States and the world could not be laid at the doorstep of Keynes.
Minsky was convinced that the key attribute he shared with Keynes

was that neither of them were Keynesians. As far as Minsky was concerned, the mainstream theorists had squeezed the life out of what Keynes had to offer. Read Minsky's monograph and you are destined to see Keynes in a new light.

Minsky highlighted the fact that Keynes, a very successful speculator in commodities, completely rejected Never Never Lander notions of well-informed and always rational investors:

> Enterprise only pretends to itself to be mainly actuated by the statements in its own prospectus. Only a little more than an expedition to the South Pole, it is based on an exact calculation of benefits to come.[1]

Minsky recognized that Keynes offered the world a theory to explain a capitalist system with *sophisticated financial institutions*. Early in this book we imagined a world without financial markets. We talked about how a boom and bust cycle could arise, a consequence of the mismatch between the way consumers save and the patterns of business investment. Paul Samuelson, the most accomplished and prolific postwar Keynesian, developed just such a model to explain business cycles, and it was the standard explanation for business cycles in the 1950s and the 1960s.[2]

Minsky's Keynesian system embraced the notion that business cycles are driven by the instability of investment. But the underlying cause, he makes quite clear, is the tenuous nature of financial relationships and the "instability of portfolios and of financial relations." Quite simply, for Minsky financial markets are center stage.

Minsky believed that boom and bust cycles are guaranteed by the interactions of the myriad players who meet and deal in the world of finance. Therefore, models for the economy that leave out banks and financial system upheavals are destined to fail.

Pervasive uncertainty rules the world. To cope with the unknown, the majority allows yesterdays to inform opinions about tomorrow. A string of happy yesterdays raises confidence in blue skies tomorrow. Risky finance gets riskier as confidence builds. In the last scene, with little margin for safety in place, a small disappointment has shockingly profound consequences.

In 1975, Minsky put it this way:

The missing step in the standard Keynesian theory [is] the explicit consideration of capitalist finance within a cyclical and speculative context . . . finance sets the pace for the economy. As recovery approaches full employment . . . soothsayers will proclaim that the business cycle has been banished [and] debts can be taken on. . . . But in truth neither the boom, nor the debt deflation . . . and certainly not a recovery, can go on forever. Each state nurtures forces that lead to its own destruction.[3]

For the cult of Wall Street fans who now dub financial crises "Minsky moments," Keynes without Minsky is something like Caesar without Shakespeare (Figure 14.1).

Why Banks and Wall Street Are Special

Schumpeter celebrated the creative destruction that he believed was the signature characteristic of a capitalist system. As he saw it, entre-preneurial risk taking was the source of long-term growth. The fact that innovation destroyed the value of established franchises was an

Figure 14.1

Tom Bachtell

inescapable part of the process. The creative destruction that Schumpeter envisioned certainly makes sense when we think of Main Street. Progress requires us to accept a never-ending string of new champions setting up shop as old peddlers give up and close their doors. For Schumpeter, *creative destruction is the price of progress.*

Naive free market apologists mistakenly see financial market crises in the same light. Arthur Laffer, a man ready to blame government intervention for meteor showers, in late 2008, put it this way:

Financial panics, if left alone, rarely cause much damage to the real economy, output, employment, and production. . . . People who buy homes and the banks who give them mortgages are no different than investors in the stock market. . . . Good decisions should be rewarded and bad decisions should be punished.[4]

In other words, we can treat a string of bank failures the same way we do a succession of fast food restaurant bankruptcies—with enthusiasm for creative destruction and a heavy dose of benign neglect.

More specifically, Fed and Treasury officials should have welcomed AIG's default, days after the Lehman bankruptcy, and whoever failed in subsequent days. Simple free market rhetoric. Simple, neat, and wrong.

Minsky's central insight is that financial companies are different. Widespread bankruptcy in the world of finance, the horrendous experience of the 1930s taught us, produces *deflationary destruction*. Ever since the 1930s, policy makers have been forced to accept that self-evident truth. And that is why, whatever their political stripes, they always end up writing any and all checks necessary to prevent a domino chain of bank and other finance company failures.

The Great Depression vs. Japan's Lost Decade

What is deflationary destruction? Contrast the dynamics of Japan in the 1990s with the fate that befell the United States in the 1930s. In both countries a wild speculative bubble took hold. Herd mentality drove the prices of stocks to levels that were completely at odds with the earnings these companies could deliver. When the bubble burst and asset prices began to plunge, banks found that the stocks and real estate and corporate loans they had made were tumbling in value.

As we explained in Chapter 3, a bank's equity at any moment is the difference between the value of its assets and the value of its liabilities. In Japan in the 1990s many bank assets fell in value by 80 percent. In the United States in the 1930s many bank assets plunged in value. On a mark-to-market basis, therefore, both banking systems were bankrupt midway through the process.

Despite these brutal similarities, the economic consequences of the bubble were wildly different. In the United States in the 1930s unemployment hit 25 percent, and industrial production fell by 40 percent. In Japan the jobless rate never climbed above 6 percent, and production fell by 10 percent and then went sideways for the next five years.

Why was Japan spared full-blown depression? Banking system survival is the key difference between Japan in the 1990s and the United States in the 1930s depression. In the United States, 9,600 banks failed. In Japan, banks limped their way through the decade, with a few forced mergers and ultimately government money to recapitalize the system. But there were no bank runs. The center held.

The visible hand of government, pure and simple, is the reason that Japan's banks survived and U.S. depression–era banks collapsed. FDIC insurance was created in the aftermath of the Great Depression. A bank run was avoided in Japan because depositors had confidence in a government guarantee.

The collapse of banks throughout America wiped out the savings of millions of Americans. The consequent plunge in their buying power drove sales, output, employment, and production into a free fall. The lesson is unambiguous. Banks are not like other businesses. The "too big to fail" doctrine has been in practice since the 1930s. Both Bush presidencies signed major bailouts into law, ideological leanings notwithstanding.

For Schumpeter, creative destruction is the price of progress. For Minsky, government activism, to thwart the deflationary effects of banking crises, is the cost of capitalism. The last 50 years of global growth and rising living standards give license to those who celebrate Schumpeter. But it is Minsky's framework that explains policy responses to financial system mayhem. We need to create a model that allows both Schumpeter's and Minsky's visions to coexist throughout the business cycle.

Systemic Risk and Modern Finance

Amidst the 2008 global market meltdown, Alan Greenspan was almost speechless. He openly confessed to being shocked by the collapse and acknowledged that at some basic level market participants had miscalculated. As he put it: "It was the failure to properly price risky assets that precipitated the crisis."[5]

But Greenspan could not bring himself to admit the obvious: the financial architecture he depended on was fundamentally flawed. Even amidst the carnage of the 2008 crisis, in his October mea culpa he guilelessly sung its praise:

> In recent decades, a vast risk management and pricing system has evolved, combining the best insights of mathematicians and finance experts supported by major advances in computer and communications technology. A Nobel prize was awarded for the discovery of the pricing model that underpins much of the advance in derivatives markets.[6]

What could have thwarted a system designed by Ayn Rand–reading rocket scientists? The "intellectual edifice . . . collapsed," Greenspan explained:

... because the data inputted into the risk management models covered a period of euphoria. Had . . . the models been fitted more appropriately to historic periods of stress, capital requirements would have been much higher and the financial world would be in far better shape today.[7]

Greenspan's conclusion?

The financial landscape that will greet the end of the crisis will be far different. . . . Investors, chastened, will be exceptionally cautious.[8]

In other words, state-of-the-art modeling, notwithstanding its mathematical prowess, is still captive to the biases that come from an extended period of happy yesterdays. Sadly, Alan Greenspan thinks the mistake was confined to the data that was *put into* the models. From Minsky's perspective, the problem is systemic. You can slice risk and dice risk and spread it all around. But you can't make it go away.

Minsky's work, therefore, runs smack up against the foundations of modern finance. Both have the same focus. Minsky was an economist wed to accounting concepts. Everyone faces a *financial survival constraint.* In other words, we need the cash we collect to match our promises to pay cash. We all have assets and liabilities. We collect cash inflows and attempt to honor our cash commitments.

Modern finance, as reflected in the "best insights of mathematicians and finance experts," to quote Greenspan, depends upon the idea that markets rationally assess future economic prospects. The system, therefore, appropriately prices risk, at any moment in time. Because Greenspan embraced that notion, he was comfortable with the breakneck pace of financial innovation around him. And he refused, quite explicitly, to lean against the winds of financial market enthusiasm.

Again, Minsky's language and arithmetic mirror modern finance concepts. But his conclusions are wildly different. Growing conviction in the enduring nature of a trend is predictable, as is the increased leverage that comes with it. But that false confidence sets the market—and its rocket scientist modelers—up for shocking disappointments.[9]

Macroeconomics, Post-Keynesians, and Behavioral Finance

Famed Yale economist Robert Shiller is not shy about criticizing the last several decades of monetary policy. He warned about irrational exuberance in the stock market in the late 1990s and waved a red flag again in 2005, focusing on the emerging bubble in housing. Professor Shiller also is on record about the shortcomings of mainstream economists:

> Why do professional economists always seem to find that concerns with bubbles are overblown or unsubstantiated? . . . It must have something to do with the tool kit given to economists (as opposed to psychologists) and perhaps even with the self-selection of those attracted to the technical, mathematical field of economics. Economists aren't generally trained in psychology. . . . They pride themselves on being rational.[10]

Behavioral economists like Professor Shiller clearly understood the dynamics that gripped asset markets in the last two decades in a way that mainstream economists did not. Shiller himself notes that "behavioral economists are still regarded as a fringe group by mainstream economists."[11]

To my way of thinking, behavioral finance, one field in behavioral economics, provides modern day insights that buttress Minsky's financial instability hypothesis. Championing the notion that mainstream theory should embrace important parts of Minsky's thesis, in effect, also amounts to ending the fringe status of behavioral finance.

Wall Street, Entrepreneurs, and Monetary Policy

Can we imagine policies that marry a celebration of risk taking with appropriate angst about systemic risks? Minsky, at least in his published work, was doubtful. He rejected the notion that monetary policy could tame capitalist instability. His skepticism about stabilization strategies and his concerns about social equity led him to champion a move toward socializing investment. I would point out, however, that Minsky was uncertain about his policy prescriptions. As he put it himself in 1986:

> Even as I warn against the hand waving that passes for much of policy prescription, I must warn the reader that I feel much more comfortable with my diagnosis of what ails our economy . . . than I do with the remedies I propose.[12]

However, even amidst the imposing shadow of the 2008 crisis, the record of free market capitalism over the past 50 years is striking. The postwar reality—good gains in living standards in the developed world—combined over the past two decades with sharp improvements in the economic circumstances of nearly 2 billion Asians. When compared to the experience of socialized investment in the former Eastern Bloc—with its waste, inefficiency, and, ultimately, indifference to the needs of its citizenry—free market capitalism triumphs, flaws and all.

Lastly, mathematicians and finance experts clearly play a central role in these accomplishments. Success in capitalist economies, history tells us, in part reflects the room to maneuver that risk takers are given. As Nicholas Kaldor, an unrepentant Keynesian put it:

> The same forces which produce violent booms and slumps will also tend to produce a high trend-rate of progress. It is the economy in which businessmen are reckless and speculative, where expectations are highly volatile but with an underlying bias toward optimism . . . [that] is likely to show a higher rate of progress, while an economy of sound and cautious business-men . . . is likely to grow at a slow rate.[13]

In short, one cannot forget that the essential driver in free market capitalism is the risk-taking entrepreneur, bankrolled by the world of finance. Enlightened societies, therefore, need to embrace free market capitalism, coupled with policies aimed at increasing margins of safety and tempering flights of fancy.

Can we regulate our way out of the problem? The overarching theme for regulatory reform has to be about instituting rules that create safety margins for the myriad nonbank financiers who arose outside the safety net created in the aftermath of the 1930s. But regulations are costly. They will only take us so far. And they will be effective for only a while. If we continue celebrating innovation—as we should—then we need to recognize that innovation on Wall Street, over time, dulls the applicability of a given set of regulations.

Minsky Modified Monetary Policy

Does Minsky's diagnosis of capitalist economies suggest a rule for central bankers that can eliminate financial system excesses and boom and bust patterns? Obviously, no. In the long-standing debate about rules versus discretion at central banks, Minsky—and any serious student of economic history—knew that no hard-and-fast rule can replace the judgment of the moment. Nonetheless, I believe strongly that central bankers armed with an appreciation of Minsky's insights can improve economic performance. To that end the simplest way to deliver streamlined monetary policy guidelines is to imagine a policy rule.

Monetary policy since the mid-1980s roughly corresponded to the Taylor rule. This critical equation directed officials to adjust short-term interest rates solely in reaction to changing inflation and unemployment. The beginning of a new strategy could come with a reworking of Taylor's famous policy rule.

This simple equation captured the essence of monetary policy discussions over the past 25 years. The Fed was being restrictive if the Fed funds rate was significantly higher than the rate of inflation. It was being very easy if the rate was lower than the inflation rate.

A Minsky retrofit of this rule would make it responsive to the potentially destabilizing swings in financial markets. Instead of simply focusing on the federal funds rate—the short-term rate controlled by the Fed—the rule should consider long-term rates on risky assets, particularly the spread between those rates and long-term rates for Treasury bonds.

As I noted throughout this book, asset bubbles swell when risk appetites are high and credit spreads are tight. Had the Fed paid more attention to credit spreads in 2004-2005, tightening would have been much more aggressive. Home prices would have cracked much earlier. And the 2008-2009 recession would probably have been milder.

Central bankers, as we saw in living color in 2008, are always at the ready to respond to violent increases in credit spreads. When stock and corporate bond markets go into free fall, policy makers ease aggressively, pointing out that investors need to be cleansed of primal fears.

And therein lay the problem. For the past 25 years policy makers were willing to say they knew better amidst falling markets, but refused to respond to rapidly rising markets. This asymmetry played a major role in the creation of a succession of asset bubbles. And much of today's crisis stems from this asymmetric response.

Ben Bernanke revealed more than perhaps he wanted to in a meeting in the fall of 2008. As the megabailout was being crafted, he reminded his colleagues that "there are no atheists in foxholes and no ideologues in financial crises."[14] Taken literally, that would suggest he believes in Schumpeter on the way up and Minsky on the way down. As I have stressed, the new paradigm requires us to somehow embrace both visionaries simultaneously.

Minsky's read of Keynes led him to focus on financial markets, risk appetites, and margins of safety as the primal causes of boom and bust cycles. We can use his insights to divine a strategy that at least somewhat reduces the risk of calamitous outcomes like the crisis of 2008. Again, however, there is simply no elixir to be had that will ensure a Goldilocks backdrop. History reminds us that one of the costs of capitalism is a periodic dose of market mayhem. The extent of financial market and real economy dislocation can be reduced if central bankers explicitly acknowledge this flaw and conduct policy with an eye toward tempering financial system excesses.

Chapter | 15

ONE PRACTITIONER'S PROFESSIONAL JOURNEY

I go to encounter for the millionth time
the reality of experience.
—James Joyce, *A Portrait of the Artist*
as a Young Man, 1916

The focus of my adult life has been on real-world puzzles. I have worked hard to understand economic theories, as a means to an end. I am not a naive free market apologist, convinced that government intervention worsens our economic opportunities at every turn. That said, I have spent the lion's share of my career marveling at the spectacular financial machinery that, most of the time, bankrolls profitable and socially advantageous endeavors. I object to activist government intervention, except in cases where it cannot be avoided. That, of course, puts me at odds with many of the most vociferous fans of Hy Minsky. What follows is a brief sketch of the experiences that led me to the prejudices that I hold.

Early Years

Most people's sensibilities are influenced by the world they inhabit as a young adult. The event that shaped my first professional aspirations was the Super Bowl victory by the New York Jets in 1969. I played high school football and dreamed about an NFL career. Talk about irrational exuberance! During saner moments I thought a lot about environmental issues. *Silent Spring* by Rachel Carson convinced me that the world was at risk. During my summer job before college I ate a bag lunch each day on the Staten Island ferry. As I stared at the Hudson River, I imagined a career as an environmental engineer—that is, after I retired from pro football.

As a freshman at Johns Hopkins, I declared my major as environmental engineering and played freshman football. Things changed. I graduated as a resource economist, sporting a championship ring in lacrosse. My sports switch was easy to understand. Playing lacrosse before 10,000 people was a lot more fun than playing football in an empty stadium.

My professional transition was a bit more complex. One of the courses required for my major was entitled Resource Management and Conservation. To take the course, I had to take a year of economics. And in 1972, I had two epiphanies, one per class.

Environmental problems, I decided, were the result of *market imperfections*, not engineering inadequacies. I soon became convinced that the fate of the world rested in the hands of economists, not engineers.

And my second epiphany? I was really good at economics! All those premed geeks who drove me crazy in freshman chemistry struggled to get C's and B's in macroeconomics. I got the highest grade on the midterm and an easy A for the course. Economics, thereafter, framed my thinking.

Microeconomic Foundations

For the most part, real-world issues in my early years involved cases where free markets failed to deliver desirable outcomes. The first energy crisis, in 1973, was precipitated by OPEC's decision to embargo oil sales. The embargo ushered in a quadrupling of oil prices, a surge for inflation, and a deep global recession. Energy economics became the rage.

Water and air pollution issues also received widespread attention. A cutlery factory bought coal and tin and electricity, paid workers, and sold spoons. Free markets were best at bringing coal and workers to the factory and selling spoons to willing buyers. But if the factory dumped mercury into a lake or stream, severe environmental damage was likely. The cost of those damages, however, was not reflected in the price of the spoon—it was, in fact, *external* to free market transactions.

My first job was as a summer intern at the Rockefeller Commission. The commission was charged with estimating the costs and benefits of instituting the environmental protection efforts mandated by the Clean Water Act amendments of 1972.

The legislation called for a three-step approach to water clean-up. Best practicable treatment was to be put in place by 1978. Best available treatment was mandated by 1980. And the last mandate? The legislation's stated goal was to achieve *zero discharge of pollutants by 1985*!

Thus, the new law called for water protection that in its early stage was practical, in its middle stage might be excessive, and in its final stage defied the law of the conservation of mass!

This led to my third epiphany. Government intervention in response to market failures delivers its own set of problems. Moreover, once the precedent of government intervention is established, you have opened up Pandora's box. What constitutes market failure? For an elected official in a tight race, all sorts of government largesse can be justified on the grounds that market outcomes are less than ideal. In the real world, it now seemed clear to me, two things were true. Free markets, in important places, fail. But once we give the green light to government action, we introduce an equally daunting set of other problems.

I concluded that a successful capitalist country needed to celebrate the invisible hand of free markets. That is the only protection a democratic society has against creeping socialism and government agencies' appetites for ever larger intrusion. But when market failure is unmistakable and its costs are large, the visible hand of government intervention will have to be brought to bear, warts and all. The Clean Water Act was far from perfect, but if you want to see Plan B, check out the water in the Huangpu River outside of Shanghai!

Macroeconomic Formulations

When thinking about the overall economy, when does government have to step in? As an economist working in the U.S. Senate in 1980, I learned firsthand. Paul Volcker's war against inflation had led him to take overnight interest rates above 20 percent. My boss, Senator Paul Tsongas from Massachusetts, was on the Banking Committee. Mutual savings banks, mostly found in Massachusetts, were on the verge of collapse. I found myself a spectator at an incredible meeting.

Speaker of the House Tip O'Neill, with some support from Senator Paul Tsongas, made the case to Paul Volcker for a change in focus at the Fed. Mutual savings banks in 1980 did not have FDIC insurance.

Given the surge for bank-borrowing costs that attended Fed-engineered 20 percent overnight interest rates, a great many mutual savings banks were on the brink of insolvency. If a few failed, the world would quickly discover the absence of FDIC insurance. Bank runs, O'Neill warned, were a genuine risk.

What happened? Over the next six months the Fed drove overnight interest rates sharply lower. By mid-1981 they stood at 10.6 percent, down nearly 1,000 basis points from their peak. Am I suggesting Volcker caved when Tip O'Neill thundered? Anyone who watched six-foot-six-inch Paul Volcker in Congressional testimony during those gut-wrenching times knows that is preposterous. What forced the Fed's hand was the growing risk to banking system safety and soundness. Thus, the simple debate about inflation/unemployment trade-offs was missing a central consideration. Banks can play a pivotal role in the Fed's decision to relent on tight money. When I made this observation to a friend, he chuckled. "You need to read Hyman Minsky!" he said. And I did.

In 1982, I left Washington to take a job at E.F. Hutton, where I became chief economist. I have spent all of the years since as the chief economist at one of four firms. That means, quite simply, that for nearly three decades I have conjured up visions of what the future will bring. How do I reconcile my deep-seated belief in *pervasive uncertainty* with 27 years of economic predictions? As I stressed in Chapter 3, all of us are in the business of strategizing about the future—an opinion about what comes next influences nearly every business and consumer decision.

Early on in my career on Wall Street, I recognized that only a select group of economists garnered much attention. Key decision makers on both Wall Street and Main Street told me why. To be of use, a true Wall Street guru has to be in the business of trying to anticipate major changes. Most important, a savvy forecaster needs to provide guidance about when things might begin to go awry.

Using Minsky's framework in tandem with a combination of financial market barometers and real economy leading indicators, I forecast recession and spectacular interest rate ease in summer 1990, spring 2000, and summer 2007. In each case, for about six months the forecast was very much at odds with the consensus outlook. Once recession took hold and ideological biases gave way to full-bore rescue efforts by governmental authorities, I wagered that Armageddon would be avoided and counseled that opportunities were now coming into view.

A purveyor of a theory based on pervasive uncertainty without a blemish on his track record? Fat chance. I did correctly call the collapse for Japan Inc. but then called for a rebound for Japan in 1996. Dead wrong, it turned out. I declared the United States to be in a technology bubble that would end in tears. But my declaration came in early 1999! Over the next 15 months, anyone who listened to me and shorted tech shares would have been crucified. When the 2001 recession proved short and shallow, I tempered, for a moment, my contentions about monetary policy errors.[1] Throughout 2005, I joined with conventional analysts and predicted rising long-term interest rates amidst Fed tightening. Thus, I too was puzzled initially by the "conundrum" that played such a central role in Alan Greenspan's final policy miscalculation.

Right Brain/Left Brain Cogitations

Nonetheless, I am proud of my track record despite a handful of brutal forecasting failures. A fair amount of the time, I was able to deliver useful input to my clients. Most important, I was willing to break with the conventional wisdom, even when that seemed at odds with the world in place, and even when it put me in dangerously lonely territory.

As I emphasized several times in this book, for unsophisticated opinion holders, belief in a big change in our immediate future arrives only after it has taken shape in the rearview mirror. What about professional economists touting large and complex forecasting models? Recall Greenspan's mea culpa in October 2008. He claimed that the financial architecture failed because the models were calibrated using data gleaned "from a period of euphoria." Macroeconomic models suffer from some of the same flawed reliance on yesterday's news. Without getting into great detail, macro forecasting models have embedded within them calculations on previous economic performance. And as a consequence, tomorrow looks like recession only after yesterday's data takes on a decidedly recessionary tone. In effect, Ma and Pa extrapolate yesterday's news, and macroeconomic models extrapolate yesterday's trends.

Beyond my comparative advantage as a reader of Minsky, what else helped me out? I teach a course at Johns Hopkins entitled The Art and Science of Economic Forecasts. The point of the course is that rigorous mathematical models are an essential tool for processing emerging information. But the *art* part, the part that makes a forecaster useful to his clients, requires a big-picture holistic judgment. Neuropsychologists would say it requires powerful right brain skills. Looking through the details of the question to get to an overarching sense of the issue is at the heart of right brain thinking.

Out of the Mouths of Babes

The best right brain thinking I have witnessed in recent years occurred outside of Toronto, at the end of a holiday weekend in 1998. At the conclusion of a hockey tournament, I was driving my eldest son and four teammates home to Connecticut. The traffic as we began the 500 mile trip was horrendous. I promised to take back roads and get us home as fast as I could. Then I offered up a challenge. "Everyone, including me, gets a piece of paper. In the next 15 minutes we all write down the time we think we will pull into my driveway. I'll put up $20. Closest guess wins it."

I felt the offer would buy me at least 15 minutes of peace in the car. And I felt safe that my computational skills would allow me to keep my $20. When we pulled into my driveway, however, I discovered I had lost—even though we arrived at home only 35 minutes later than I had predicted. I lost to my son. His piece of paper read as follows:

> We'll arrive a few minutes after Dad predicts. He is great at forecasting, but he's always a little too optimistic.

One Picture Can Be Worth a Thousand Equations

In an earlier chapter I highlighted the painful miscalculations that led a majority of analysts in 2001 to believe that the future would deliver a $5 trillion U.S. budget surplus. I never bought the swelling surplus story.

I had spent 30 years watching elected officials fight tooth and nail over taxing and spending decisions. How could it be true that a multi-trillion-dollar bounty was scheduled to arrive, essentially out of thin air? In the book *A Beautiful Mind,* John Forbes Nash, Jr., explained that his best insights came to him *before he could do the math that proved them.* Similarly, I was convinced the $5 trillion surplus story was fanciful. I simply had to find the fatal flaws in the argument.

The standard explanation for the surging surplus was straightforward. The U.S. economy was booming, a consequence of booming technology-driven gains in productivity. These gains were likely to continue. Recessions, if they arrived, would be mild. Major military conflicts had been relegated to history, thanks to the end of the cold war. In short, conventional analysts were comfortable forecasting an extension of the heady world that had unfolded in 1995-2000.

A part of my time in Washington had been spent as an economist in the Congressional Budget Office. I called down to CBO. They were confident in the forecast. On Wall Street it was embraced completely. As one booster of the story put it to me, "You can't make the surplus go away, Bob. To do so you would have to forecast next to no growth for the next decade." For me, his utterance was the eureka moment. It simply could not be true that only a decade of dismal economic performance could derail the surplus story. And I soon figured out why.

Take a good look at the chart in Figure 15.1. It is a picture that completely debunks the notion that the late 1990s surge in government revenues was driven by a booming U.S. economy. Economic growth had been good over the period. But the boom in revenues, as the chart shows, reflected an unmistakable explosion in tax revenues as a share of the overall economy. For reasons that the CBO admitted it did not understand, tax receipts had grown 11 percent per year, nearly double the growth rate for nominal GDP—the economy's overall spending rate. Personal tax receipts, as a consequence, had climbed to 10.2 percent of GDP, wildly above the postwar average of 8.5 percent. And they stood at a level that was unprecedented relative to any other period in the postwar years!

I then made a straightforward observation:

Figure 15.1

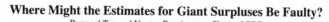

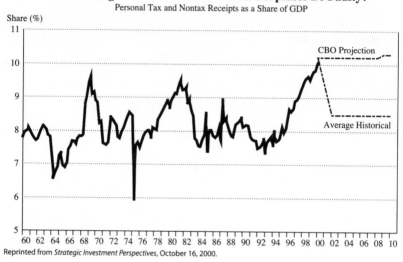

Where Might the Estimates for Giant Surpluses Be Faulty?
Personal Tax and Nontax Receipts as a Share of GDP

Reprinted from *Strategic Investment Perspectives,* October 16, 2000.

If over the next two years personal tax receipts relative to GDP were to fall back to 8.5 percent, the CBO's estimate for the 2002 surplus would be overstated by $185 billion.[2]

Why might tax receipts plunge as a share of GDP? I was able to document that the late 1990s leap reflected capital gains and options exercises. In other words, the surge in receipts reflected the Nasdaq bubble. As I wrote in an editorial for the *Financial Times* in October 2000:

> Close examination of the assumptions made . . . suggests that estimates for the future size of the federal surplus are wildly optimistic. . . . Much of the better than expected revenue gains . . . have been tied to the stock market. . . . The risk is that

receipts on capital gains and options income will fall sharply in the years ahead. The bubble economy has created a bubble budget.[3]

As we all now know, it turned out to be much worse than I imagined. The stock market bubble burst. And we had both a recession and a war. But in the fall of 2000, I was able to claim that one picture was worth 1,000 equations. Glance again at Figure 15.1 and it becomes clear that the 2001 vision of a $5 trillion surplus was always a mirage.

At the time, however, it was definitely not the conventional wisdom. Indeed, several analysts accused me of not understanding tax accounting. Floyd Norris, in a *New York Times* blog in the fall of 2008, put it this way:

> . . . It is too bad that more people did not realize then that the budget surplus forecasts that justified big tax cuts were based on bad assumptions about tax receipts. . . . My colleague Paul Krugman, in criticizing Mr. Greenspan . . . argues that the tax cuts were "based on budget projections that everyone knew, even then, were wildly overoptimistic."
>
> I disagree. I thought they were overoptimistic, but that was not the conventional wisdom. In 2000, the Congressional Budget Office (under Republican control) came up with a huge forecasted surplus, and the Office of Management and Budget (under Democratic control) agreed.
>
> In October 2000, I wrote a column, quoting Robert Barbera, now the chief economist of ITG, making the point that the surpluses were based on assumptions of an ever-rising stock market. . . . It was a message few wanted to hear. . . . Mr. Greenspan did

not see the problem coming, but he was far from alone in that regard.[4]

Hindsight is 20/20. Ask analysts in 2008 about the $5 trillion surplus story and you will probably be told that they knew it was too good to be true. To object in 2001, however, you needed a large dose of skepticism and a willingness to champion a chart as your rebuttal to overwhelmingly detailed forecasting formulations.

And Finally, a Healthy Dose of James Joyce Comes in Handy

H. G. Wells wrote a letter to James Joyce soon after the publication of *Ulysses*, deriding Joyce's classic work. He accused Joyce of modeling a world trapped in never-ending cycles. Joyce's next creation, *Finnegan's Wake*, is precisely that. Joyce has an Irish bartender fall asleep and conjure all European history in a flow of insight and invented language that begins where it ends. A blueprint for presenting the U.S. political business cycle? On vacation in the early 1990s, after chatting for too long with my own bartender, I began to think so. And the editorial board of the *Wall Street Journal*, happily for me, agreed. On Election Day 1992, as George Bush lost the White House to Bill Clinton, the *Journal's* editorial page carried my parody of *Finnegan's Wake* (Figure 15.2). There are no equations, language is invented, and there is a dash of tragic irony. I like to think of it as a model that has some heft despite minimal formal structure. For me, the art part of economics is what makes it both funny and sad.

Figure 15.2

THE WALL STREET JOURNAL.

TUESDAY, NOVEMBER 3, 1992

The Economy According to Joyce

Nearly half a century ago James Joyce completed his epic "Finnigans Wake." The experimental novel, replete with pun-filled and invented language, presented the world from the point of view of a sleeping Irish barkeeper. Below, Robert J. Barbera, chief economist and a managing director at Lehman Bros., tries his hand at a modern-day look at the economy in the style of the master:

moneyrun, past ease and add'em, from splurge at store to lend at bank, brings us by a commodius vicus of reliquification to White House and Environs.

Sir Grnspnsham had as passenger North Armorica, where he'd wielded his preciprice war and promised gorgeous-growthstreams; not yet though venisoon

Joyce Contemplates the Numbers

after, then had a deerscad of a clintonlad claim Dem's efforts were worth more than twobushes. The consequent fall of a once grand oldpa is retaled herein, amid a vision thing or two, by recounting the old electiooneer parable.

The Death of the GOPse And the Debt Gripes

Eighties was a place and a creditwide place it was ere ruled a GOPse. His onesomeness was alltomanly, archand-

posing, ovaloffice, and a GOPse he would a photop go (my heli!cried Giorgio Ronaldo). so one latesummer evening, after absorbing great credit amid his good supper of commies and irakish, having flattend the reds, freed the thrifts, defeated the Dukes of Kakis, and saddamized the desert storms, he put on his impermeable, seized his impugnable, harped on his crown stepped out of his immobile Chey Maison Blanco and set off for mainstreet to see how gladness was gladness in the splashiest of all expensible ways.

As he set off with his father's sword, his Raygun raisondettra, he clanked to my clinking, from Veepee to buck stop, every inch of a twelve-year incumbent.

But no sooner did he come upon the bridge between memoriamalls and shopping spreedom, then was he dumbfoundered as he gazed upon the most unconscionably dead in the water spending stream he ever locked eyes with. It trickled down little and it flowed less and it acted narrow and it rose showshallow. And as it limped it wafted in creeky creepy voice: my my my!me and me!Little lift here I won't carry thee!

And Dem's declare, what was there weighing on yonder banks of the stagnant stream that would be a recovery but the debt gripes. In all his specious heavings, as be levered by optimist maximus, the GOPse had never seen his dumbville spenders-on-low so nigh to an election.

Good day to you, sir GOPse! Squeezed the gripes in a debt laden line. Pin no hopes on rising currents if you please. For I am obliged to weigh heavy, and whine for a lot more than you give me credit for.

Rates! Bullowed the GOPse, as he lowered the fundsboomer time and again. Blast yourself and your interest in payments. Excite yourself upon my new world order. Cry me a rivcovery if you pull ease. Gripes however would have

none of it. But you kind sour are indebted to US. And I regret to proclaim that US liabilites assure you'll miss liftoff by inches. And of course the sad truth was that with such a thrust of an argument there was simply no room for leverage. For you cannot quake a milkenedhouse out of a lent ear.

Twas true, gripes had come to bury Caesar not appraise him. And as the year rolled by the gripes held tight despite cashcading all the time, the short interest slide and ride rated wildest ever wielded. At last in desperation our August GOPse tried breaking with convention and employyed his subjects to look beyond their gripes: the new world's taken order, forget what's owed and let my tenure flow. Only after your nomember, delevered the gripes! And the gripes not the GOPse made good on his delevery. For twasnt till nomember GOPse greeped silently, no charge, away.

All me life I have lived above them, but now they loath me. I was kind and gentle when I came into view. I could of stayed up there forever. Only. Its something fails us. First we run. Then we fall. . . .

Yes! and then the gripes, too, began to lose its grip, and slip, and soon the banks were awash in new greenery, amid a lifting of gloom to glidder times.

And thus it was, eversolate but ever so visible, with banks over brimming in cash, grand oldpa gone, and a newly minted clint in everyone's eyes, we arrived at the sight of salvXLRation. Too late for bushes, but bursting dollops from its banks nonetheless.

Yes! Quitealive, yes. There's where. We pass through cash, we're flush, then, whush! A glow, wow. Far calls. Coming far. US then. A rise again! Awakened too. A way a loan at last a lift a long the

— New York, Nantucket, Greenwich, 1992.

Chapter | 16

GLOBAL POLICY RISKS IN THE AFTERMATH OF THE 2008 CRISIS

It's supposed to be hard. If it wasn't hard, everyone would do it.
The hard . . . is what makes it great!

—Jimmy Dugan, as played by Tom Hanks,
A League of Their Own, 1992

Much of this book is about the need to accept capitalism's obvious flaws. Evidence over the past 25 years supports the notion that confidence in a self-correcting economy turns out to be misplaced. Economic theory and central bank practice need to be recast in this light. But this book also embraces the upside of market-driven economies. And it could well turn out that the emerging risk to economic prosperity in the years ahead will involve a loss of confidence in the very foundations of free markets. Thus, we now probably will face assaults on compromise strategies from both the right and the left.

In this final chapter, I will summarize the case made throughout the book. I will use that framework to sketch out the rationale for big government rescue efforts in 2009. Finally, I will conjecture about what I see as threats to economic prosperity in the years beyond the current economic crisis.

The Dynamic Restated

Risk appetites grow as good times endure. Borrowing costs for uncertain endeavors retreat, asset markets climb, and increasingly risky finance proliferates. Late in an expansion, the financial system balances on a precipice. In the end a small setback on Main Street kicks off serious financial market dislocations, which then reverberate in the real economy. The full scope of economic retrenchment dwarfs the expectations of those who took comfort in the fact that imbalances on Main Street were modest. Enlightened central bankers, as a consequence, need to be willing to lean against the wind of rising risk appetites in recognition of the destabilizing nature of financial system excesses.

The Dynamic in a Global Context and the Need for a New Consensus

The upswing in asset prices that ultimately ended in a deep recession during the Asian contagion of the late 1990s was driven by foreign capital inflows from the developed world. Greenspan's conundrum— falling borrowing costs for most Americans despite stepwise Federal Reserve Board tightening—can be looked at as the triumph of easy money in China over tightening attempts by the U.S. central bank. The fact that European banks in the 2008 crisis suffered almost the same fate as U.S. banks drove home the interconnected nature of the world's financial system.

Thus, from a global perspective, central bankers face two problems. They need to lean against the wind of rising risk appetites. But tailwinds emanating from foreign capital inflows may compromise their efforts. History tells us that policy coordination is achievable, but only during crises.

Therefore, the path to better monetary policy will require a new consensus on the basic responsibilities of central bankers. A worldwide commitment to keeping inflation low emerged in the aftermath of the Great Inflation of the 1970s. Central bankers, in the aftermath of the 2008 crisis, need to acknowledge that potential asset market excesses require the same attention that wage and price excesses were given as we entered the 1980s.

Economic Theory Ain't Beanbag

There is little chance that central bankers will independently devise a new strategy to respond to risk appetites and asset markets. Mainstream economic theory must first be recast. It is naive to think that the right theory can keep the wolf perpetually at bay. Financial market mayhem, as I stressed throughout this book, is an inescapable part of capitalism. But the colossal scope of the 2008 global crisis, and the severe tangible costs that the world is now paying, came into being in large part because of misguided notions about economic fundamentals. More simply, the roots of the 2008 financial markets crisis can be found in mainstream economic theory and in the mathematical architecture of modern finance. Accordingly, economic theoreticians need to suspend mathematical high jinks and concentrate on forging a new consensus, one that squares with economic reality.

The new consensus must explicitly acknowledge that *the transmission mechanism for monetary policy is through the financial markets.* The vast majority of economists, of course, know that this is the case. But this self-evident truth must become a cornerstone of macroeconomic thinking. Defenders of the ruling economic orthodoxy can point to countless papers that address any and every economic condition. Nonetheless, the mainstream framework taught to undergraduates, and the simplified model that policy makers traffic in, gives second-tier status to Wall Street. That tradition must end.

A superstylized version of how the economy works must include the interplay between central banks, asset markets, and Main Street. If standard models acknowledge the brutally obvious—that risky company borrowing rates and the cost to raise capital in equity markets go a long way toward defining the level of ease or restrictiveness in an economy—then theory will make handicapping monetary policy more straightforward. If overnight interest rates are rising but financial conditions are getting easier—as was clearly the case in 2004 and 2005—then there can be no confusion about the emerging policy circumstances. Policy is becoming more accommodative, irrespective of the alleged intentions of the central bank and the climbing trajectory for overnight rates.

Elevating financial markets to center stage for mainstream theorists will be relatively easy. Acknowledging that capital markets have a major flaw will do much more damage to conventional models. The sociological dynamic that drives risk attitudes in a world that is always uncertain must become a part of the new consensus. Sadly, for the profession, the damage done by acknowledging this self-evident truth has been done before. As I noted a few chapters back, in economics we are in the embarrassing habit of *rediscovering* truths. In current circumstances, we need to reread John Maynard Keynes with Hyman Minsky as our guide. New insights from behavioral finance must become a central part of the mainstream formulation. The simple truth is that theorists owe this to the policy-making world. The sooner they deliver it, the better.

Cushioning the Blow of the Great Debt Unwind

When deep recession takes hold, asset market excesses are distant memories. For policy makers, the front and center challenge is twofold: to stem the downward spiral for the global financial markets and to limit the damage to the worldwide economy. Government officials confront a plunging appetite for risk taking by households and businesses. And policy makers also must grapple with a sweeping desire to reduce reliance on debt to finance future endeavors. In short, no one wants to take any chances, and everyone wants to raise savings rates.

In the 1930s, Keynes taught economists that a mass move toward frugality is bound to fail. If everyone is trying to save, falling demand drives production, employment, and income sharply lower. The consequent carnage on Main Street reinforces worries on Wall Street, and asset markets face additional selling. Only aggressive government and central bank action can derail this adverse feedback loop. The protests we saw late in 2008 about the intrusion of government into the private sector are disingenuous at best and, if taken seriously, dangerously counterproductive. Why not let market declines and bankruptcies run their course? We tried that approach in the 1930s, and results were horrific.

A central focus of this book is that it is time to come to grips with how people, en masse, change their attitudes about risk taking and debt usage. In the brutal swoon that grips the world in 2009, it is critically important that we recognize how people's risk attitudes are likely to evolve. What led to the violent rise in household indebtedness over the 2000-2007 period (see Figure 16.1)? Clearly it was widespread conviction about rising house prices. In like fashion, powerful anxieties

Figure 16.1

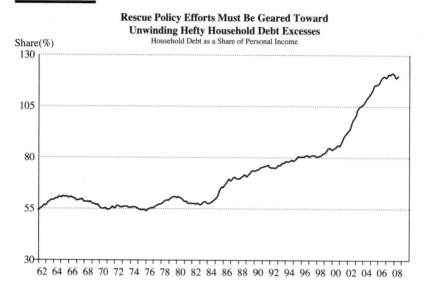

**Rescue Policy Efforts Must Be Geared Toward
Unwinding Hefty Household Debt Excesses**
Household Debt as a Share of Personal Income

about falling home prices are certain to lead many Americans to attempt to lower their debt levels over the next several years. Aggressive government policies aimed at stabilizing the housing market make good sense. Likewise, for many households a cut in taxes will allow them to raise savings rates without cutting their spending.

The Visible Government Hand Attempts to Stabilize the Housing Market

What about the argument that traditional market forces will drive residential real estate to a healthy new equilibrium? This naively denies the irrational and insane run-up for house prices that unfolded in 2001-2006 in the United States and in many developed world housing markets. Left to their own devices, the various world housing markets would fall into deep depression. That's because of the dysfunctional state of affairs that now grips the world of housing finance.

Furthermore, broad-based governmental efforts to stem the slide for home prices, coming as they do after three years of rapid decline, will not prevent home values from returning to reasonable levels. Given trends in place in late 2008, in 2009 the median home price in the United States will have fallen by nearly 35 percent in real terms. That would return home prices to values that can be supported by average buyers using conventional financing. Efforts to slow foreclosure procedures and lower home mortgage interest rates are justified, because they offer us a chance at preventing an unnecessary and extremely costly overshoot on the downside—for home prices, consumer spending, and overall economic performance.

Similarly, cutting personal income taxes frees up available cash for households. It is probably true that a fair amount of this increased cash flow will be saved. But with a tax rebate in hand, the powerful desire to increase savings can be met, in part, without cutting back on current spending. The hope has to be that a large reduction in mortgage rates catalyzes a refinancing surge. A combination of tax rebates and lower monthly mortgage payments can then allow for a rise in household savings, a reduction in debt levels, *and* only modest additional retrenchment for U.S. household spending. None of these policies is meant to return U.S. consumers to the role of global borrowers and spenders of last resort. Instead, aggressive government intervention in the United States is directed toward accommodating the urgent need for households to deleverage without imposing wild further declines on U.S. and global economic activity.

Profligate Savers Also Must Change Their Stripes

The collapse for housing prices in the developed world and the deep spending retrenchment that has taken hold in the United States and Europe is wreaking havoc on industrial export giants, including and especially China, Germany, and Japan. All three nations have run large trade surpluses and have high personal savings rates. All have been the beneficiaries of U.S. spending largess. It is almost impossible to imagine that Washington efforts can re-create the U.S. spending machine that drove the last leg of the global boom that began in the early 1980s. Indeed, as I noted earlier in the book, U.S. spending was stoked by super low mortgage rates and soaring home prices— with the low rates a consequence of the Asian central bank's buying of Treasuries that thwarted Fed efforts to slow things down.

The China boom is faltering as this book goes to print. It is destined to crumble as developed world demand for Chinese goods shrinks. China, therefore, is compelled to replace its export and investment-to-support export boom with a broad, sweeping increase in social infrastructure spending. Similarly, both Germany and Japan will need to find a way to manufacture home-grown growth, or suffer deep and protracted economic declines.

Anticipating Battle Lines in the Next War?

Arming central bankers with a new construct, this book argues, is essential. Several years back, when I suggested these changes, critics, in general, attacked from the right. Markets know best, I was told. Capital flows, risk spreads, and equity markets recalibrate in real time and will send money to the right places. Central banks need only tend to their knitting—keeping inflation low—and the rest will work itself out.

But the crisis of confidence that the world confronts as I write this final chapter suggests that the assault on a compromise capitalist strategy, over the decade to come, will emanate from the left. A willingness to engage in much more government control will be the likely result of the crisis of 2008.

The loss of confidence certainly has no parallel in my lifetime. Obviously, much of that despair reflects the simple but brutal economic and financial market facts that have come to pass in 2008. Bear Stearns gone. Lehman Brothers gone. Major money center banks receiving massive government infusions. All three U.S. auto companies pleading for government assistance and fighting for their lives. On Main Street, joblessness is soaring, and sales are in sharp retreat. And these scenes are being repeated around the globe. Ominously, for the first time in postwar history, the generalized price level is falling. In sum, as 2008 came to a close, the world confronted an unprecedented financial crisis and evidence of the onset of a deep economic decline.

For me, however, the nature of the current panic extends beyond economic and financial market realities. At some visceral level people around the world know that the simple ideology that informed decisions has failed us. Market values that were calibrated using state-of-the-art theories and lightning-fast computers collapsed in a heap. Policy makers scrambled to respond, using ad hoc tactics. Business leaders, dazed and confused, are cutting back, left, right, and center. You can almost sense a broad sweeping question.

How does one move forward if the old map is in error?

As I sketched out a few pages back, the answer to that question, for a few years, will be on the backs of big government. In the United States, infrastructure spending will climb, and subsidies for companies, from cars to solar cell makers, will mushroom. In Europe, the same will be the rule. On a grand scale, in China, government spending on hospitals, roads, and schools for the 800 million who remain in poverty will replace the great export manufacturing boom as the engine for advance in the world's most populous nation. Everywhere, government-backed economic endeavors will dominate in a way they have not since collective efforts across nations financed World War II.

The good news, as I see it, is that these efforts will likely succeed, in the sense that they will prevent the 2008 crisis from throwing the world into a full-blown global depression. But that success may well feed the forces for a generalized embrace of government-driven investment. And that, I believe, would be a major error.

Rekindling Faith in Finance

For several years leading up to the crisis of 2008, many champions of free market capitalism warned about the tenuous nature of the global credit markets. Warren Buffett, the sage of Omaha, labeled the markets impenetrable, and therefore fraught with incalculable risk. But free-flowing capital markets and the strong growth that they financed gave rise to the long string of successes that were celebrated throughout the 1990s and into the middle years of the first decade of the new millennium. Signing off on a world of slow growth, with bloated governments and a general distrust for free markets, would be tantamount to throwing the baby out with the bathwater.

For finance to reclaim its central role in modern economies, it will need to return to simpler, transparent formulations. If the math is beyond the average investor, the investment vehicle will have no role to play. Likewise, regulators will need to declare that the analysis they confront is straightforward and that they are comfortable with the paper being issued. Importantly, central bankers will need to assure the world of investors that they stand at the ready to lean against the wind of future enthusiasms in order to limit the extent of late cycle busts.

But with regulations revamped, offerings streamlined and easy to contemplate, and central bankers at the ready, elected officials will need to declare that it is once again safe to take risks in private capital markets. If instead we severely limit the role of entrepreneurs and their capitalist financiers, we will certainly prevent a 2008-style capital markets crisis. But the vast sweep of history also suggests that we will have locked ourselves into a slow-growth, low expectation universe.

I stated at the outset of this book that appropriate policy changes tied to a revamping of economic orthodoxy are needed to prevent mammoth crises. That said, it may well turn out that a renewed commitment to free market capitalism, from chastened and wiser government leaders, will give us our best chance for prosperity in the twenty-first century.

NOTES

Chapter 1

1. Hyman Minsky, *Stabilizing an Unstable Economy* (New York: McGraw-Hill, 2008), p. 199.

Chapter 3

1. Comment made on the *Charlie Rose* show, Wednesday, October 1, 2008.

Chapter 4

1. In general, household savings rates do not change quickly in aggregate. Individual families may make big changes, but that smooths out over large numbers. Yet firms are different. Investment tends not to be smooth, but very lumpy. And when a big project looks promising to one company, the chances are that it will look promising to many.

2. It also affects the return that companies are prepared to pay the households for their savings.

3. Timing issues are also affected by the random nature of technical discoveries and innovations in production.

4. Does this mean that a small group of people who "get the joke" about the inevitability of business cycle downturns can make easy money by betting against the ignorant? No. Making big bets in the marketplace is like comedy—the number one thing you need is timing. In 1999, Julian

Robertson, a very famous hedge fund guru, was convinced that technology stocks were in a wild bubble. He was adamant that their rise had to reverse. And he was convinced that once they began to fall, a recession would quickly take hold. One could argue that he was equipped with the insight that Never Never Landers are born with. Julian Robertson, however, fought with the masses for over a year—and lost. In early 2000 he closed his hedge fund, after suffering brutal losses due to his shorting of technology stocks. Over the next two years, those shares fell by 85 percent. But that was cold comfort for Julian and investors in the Tiger Fund. They were decimated by less clever trend followers, despite their savvy assessment of the situation at hand.

5. Greenspan endorsed projections that envisioned a complete payoff of the U.S. federal debt. He warned that surplus dollars collected after the debt was paid off would force the Federal Reserve Board to buy private assets in order to conduct open market operations. He shuddered at the prospect of government technocrats buying stocks or real estate in a world where all U.S. Treasury debt was paid off.

6. Testimony of Chairman Alan Greenspan, Outlook for the Federal Budget and Implications for Fiscal Policy, before the Committee on the Budget, U.S. Senate, January 25, 2001.

7. Bernanke's comments on the budget deficit were contained in a written response to questions raised by Senator Robert Menendez (D-N.J.) after the Fed chief's appearance at a Congressional hearing on the economy in February.

8. Bernanke, Outlook for the U.S. Economy Before the Joint Economic Committee, U.S. Congress, April 27, 2006.

9. Even during periods in which policy makers declare that they are attempting to engineer a change, and periods in which shocks occur to the economic system, usually only a hand is waved in the direction of the threatened change.

Chapter 5

1. Orville Schell, *Discos and Democracy*, p. 39.

2. Joseph Schumpeter, *Capitalism, Socialism, and Democracy*, pp. 84-86.

3. "A + B = C," *Strategic Investment Perspectives*, ITG Economics Research, January 22, 2008.

Chapter 6

1. His successor, Ben Bernanke, has also come under fire. Ironically, however, in 2008 Bernanke critics on Wall Street toned down their epithets. Early in Bernanke's term, when things began to look rocky, they agreed that "Greenspan would have prevented this." But the wholesale reversal of opinion about Greenspan changed the tenor of Bernanke-bashing. In the new story line, Bernanke shared some of the blame for 2008 financial system mayhem. But Alan Greenspan was the bigger sinner.

2. In Chapter 13, I point out that a very influential group of economists, new classical economists, argue that Fed policy cannot effect real growth. I also make it clear that I think this notion is nonsense.

Chapter 7

1. When people lend money, they want to be paid interest, over and above the inflation rate. If inflation is 10 percent, one year later you will need $1,100 just to buy the same amount of stuff. So you'll demand compensation beyond inflation. Economists call the payment you receive over and above inflation the "real rate."

2. Standard capital markets theory says that the value of a share of equity reflects opinions about the company's future earnings *and* the interest rate used to discount that stream of earnings to the present. Thus, the sharp fall for rates raised the discounted value of earnings, lifting stocks.

3. This regulatory arrangement had profound implications for U.S. monetary policy and for the U.S. economy. Late in expansions, every four to six years, inflationary pressures would begin to appear. Fed policy

makers, in response, would raise interest rates. Rising deposit rates would quickly pull money out of thrifts, and they would curtail lending. And since the thrift industry was by far the biggest provider of home mortgages, housing activity would violently reverse. As Figure 10.1 (in Chapter 10) shows, the housing market was wildly cyclical from 1960 through the early 1980s. The violent boom and bust cycle visible in the 1960-1970 U.S. economy in large part reflected this dynamic. For Fed policy makers, it suggested they possessed an on/off switch, not a volume control. When they raised rates, a bust ensued. Tweaking rates to slow things down was a nonstarter in this highly regulated world.

4. I sell you the bond and tell you the company is good for the money. You hold the bond, and I collect a fee. All the incentive is in place for me to get lax on my assessment of the safety of the bond, since you now have it and I've already collected my fees. This moral hazard would be repeated with a vengeance in the subprime mortgage market in the early years of the new century.

5. Only a quarter of forecasters in the summer 1990 Philadelphia FRB economic survey expected a recession over the quarters ahead.

Chapter 8

1. Japanese stocks kept falling, irregularly, for almost 20 years, hitting a new low in 2008.

2. As we will learn in Chapter 10, the developed world housing boom, and the crisis of 2008, reflected to a meaningful degree the reverse of the late 1990s—Asian dollars flooding the developed world with easy money. In that sense, although the United States had recourse, you can argue that the 2008 crisis is simply emerging Asia returning the favor.

Chapter 9

1. In late April 2000, I coauthored a more elaborate paper with Paul DeRosa of Mt. Lucas Partners. We demonstrated that the 1996-2000 boom, to continue for another 10 years, required, quite impossibly, that the unemployment rate fall into negative territory. It also necessitated a

rise for the current account deficit to 18 percent of GDP. We then dismissed the notion that profits could rise as a share of GDP, to accommodate profit forecasts within a reasonable overall macroeconomic picture. Profits would have to rise to 31 percent on national income. We pointed out that the corporate investment needed to absorb those funds was impossible to imagine. We went on to say that the political economic arithmetic of a move toward 31 percent of income going to capital rendered this scenario equally moot. ("It Just Happened Again," 11th Annual Symposium in Honor of Hyman Minsky.)

2. *Strategic Investment Perspectives*, March 13, 2000.

Chapter 10

1. Robert J. Barbera, Ph.D., Testimony before Congress, Hearing on the U.S. Trade Deficit, December 10, 1999.

2. *Strategic Investment Perspectives*, ITG Economics Research 2006.

Chapter 11

1. In a research report I wrote in 2005, I warned about the risk of this eventuality. See "Will Greenspan's Conundrum Become Bernanke's Calamity?" *Strategic Investment Perspectives*, ITG Economics Research 2005.

2. Frederick Mishkin, Housing and the Monetary Transmission Mechanism, Finance and Economics Discussion Series, Divisions of Research & Statistics and Monetary Affairs Federal Reserve Board, Washington, D.C., August 2007.

3. Federal Reserve Board Chairman Bernanke, October 31, 2008, UCLA symposium.

4. Hyman Minsky, *John Maynard Keynes*, pp. 124-25.

Chapter 12

1. They received something less than $10 per share, hardly more than a token for a company that 12 months earlier had been worth more than $175 per share.

2. My concerns about Lehman were purely professional, not personal. It is true that Lehman had employed me for eight years as its chief economist. But I was installed in that job by Shearson management, in charge of Shearson-Lehman, when it acquired E.F. Hutton.

Chapter 13

1. The microeconomic foundations of a macroeconomic response are, of course, important. Nonetheless I would submit that an undue fascination with the micro underpinnings of economywide questions has contributed to years of misguided pursuits by mainstream economic theorists.

2. Paul Samuelson, "Lord Keynes and the General Theory," *Econometrica*, vol. 4, no. 3 (1946), pp. 187-200.

3. Monetarists, more specifically, declared that the central bank's only job was to control the money supply. Controlling growth in the money supply would, in turn, deliver trajectories for inflation and employment that were as stable as possible.

4. Volcker was an opportunist when it came to monetarism. On numerous occasions in the early 1980s he adjusted his targets for money growth downward. This allowed him to keep raising interest rates until inflation cracked. But it made homage to the money targets a bit silly. Whatever money did, rates were going up until inflation went down.

5. As a staffer in Washington in 1981, I sat in a committee hearing in which Larry Kudlow, then the chief economist of OMB, presented the Reagan administration's forecast for real growth and inflation in 1981 and 1982. Inflation, Kudlow explained, would plunge, a consequence of the Fed's commitment to keep money growth low. The real economy would boom, thanks to Reagan tax cuts. How could one foot on the brake and one foot on the accelerator be counted on to deliver such an ideal outcome? Easy, according to Kudlow. Since MV = GDP, we will have a surge in V. In other words, rational expectations would

collapse inflation without requiring any real economy redress. Ingenious arithmetic, but very poor forecast.

6. The rational expectations school was monetarism on steroids. It was followed by the time consistency literature—monetarism on crack cocaine. This extension argued that the mere fact that discretion exists makes us all worse off. The math became increasingly complex, the arguments more contrived. The punch line never changed: we are all better off if discretion is eliminated and policy is set by a rule.

7. Real business cycle conclusions are simple to grasp. The models that buttress the theories are impenetrable to all but a select group of mathematically gifted, and in most cases extremely sheltered, economists.

8. Some real business types moderated this claim. The revised assertion is that any effect that monetary policy has on the economy is inefficient. If unemployment is high, the Fed can act to lower it, but this will force folks back to work from vacations they were enjoying.

9. Joseph E. Stiglitz, "Information and the Change in the Paradigm in Economics," Prize Lecture, Columbia Business School, Columbia University, December 8, 2001.

10. Washington Taylor, professor of physics, Web site, MIT.

11. Keynes, *The Collected Writings*, vol. XIV, p. 121.

Chapter 14

1. John Maynard Keynes, *The General Theory of Employment, Interest, and Money*, 1936.

2. Paul Samuelson, "Interactions Between the Multiplier Analysis and the Principal of Acceleration," *Review of Economics and Statistics*, 1939.

3. Hyman Minsky, *John Maynard Keynes*, p. 126.

4. Arthur Laffer, *The Wall Street Journal*, October 27, 2008.

5. Committee of Government Oversight and Reform, Testimony, Dr. Alan Greenspan, October 23, 2008, p. 3.

6. Ibid., p. 3.

7. Ibid.

8. Ibid., p. 4.

9. Perry Mehrling in a brilliant essay argues that the modern day debate between government interventionists and free marketers needs to be waged now between disciples of Minsky and believers in modern finance. See "Minsky and Modern Finance," *Journal of Portfolio Management*, Winter 2000.

10. Robert J. Shiller, "Challenging the Crowd in Whispers, Not Shouts," *The New York Times*, November 2, 2008.

11. Ibid.

12. Minsky, *Stabilizing an Unstable Economy*, p. 319.

13. Nicholas Kaldor, *Essays on Economic Stability and Growth*, 1960.

14. *The New York Times*, September 21, 2008.

Chapter 15

1. Robert J. Barbera, "Boom, Gloom, and Excess," *International Economy*, 2002.

2. "America's Bubble Budget," *Financial Times* editorial, October 27, 2000.

3. Ibid.

4. Floyd Norris in a *New York Times* blog in fall 2008.

REFERENCES

Books

Alcaly, Roger. *The New Economy: What It Is, How It Happened, and Why It Is Likely to Last.* New York: Farrar, Straus and Giroux, 2003.

Arnold, Lutz G. *Business Cycle Theory.* New York: Oxford University Press, 2002.

Barnett, Harold J., and Chandler Morse. *Scarcity and Growth: The Economics of Natural Resource Availability.* Baltimore: The Johns Hopkins Press, 1952.

Baumol, William J. *The Free-Market Innovation Machine: Analyzing the Growth Miracle of Capitalism.* Princeton: Princeton University Press, 2002.

Bernstein, Peter L. *Against the Gods: The Remarkable Story of Risk.* John Wiley & Sons, 1996.

DeSoto, Hernando. *The Mystery of Capital: Why Capitalism Triumphs in the West and Fails Everywhere Else.* New York: Basic Books, 2000.

Dimson, Elroy, Paul Marsh, and Mike Staunton. *Triumph of the Optimists: 101 Years of Global Investment Returns.* Princeton: Princeton University Press, 2002.

El-Erian, Mohamed. *When Markets Collide: Investment Strategies for the Age of Global Economic Change.* New York: McGraw-Hill, 2008.

Friedman, Milton and Rose. *Free to Choose: A Personal Statement*. New York: Harcourt Brace Jovanovich, 1980.

Gilder, George. *Wealth and Poverty*. New York: Basic Books, 1981.

Goetzmann, William N., and Roger G. Ibbotson. *The Equity Risk Premium: Essays and Explorations*. New York: Oxford University Press, 2006.

Grant, James. *Money of the Mind: Borrowing and Lending in America from the Civil War to Michael Milken*. New York: Farrar, Straus and Giroux, 1992.

Hansen, Alvin H. *A Guide to Keynes*. New York: McGraw-Hill, 1953.

Hicks, J. R. *Value and Capital*. Oxford: Oxford University Press, 1946.

Hutton, Will. *The Writing on the Wall: China and the West in the 21st Century*. New York: The Free Press, 2006.

Kaldor, Nicholas. *Essays on Economic Stability and Growth*. New York: Holmes & Meier, 1960.

Keynes, John Maynard. *The General Theory of Employment, Interest, and Money*. New York: Harvest/HBJ Book, 1964.

Kindleberger, Charles P. *Essays in History: Financial, Economic, Personal*. Ann Arbor: University of Michigan Press, 2002.

————. *Manias, Panics, and Crashes: A History of Financial Crises*. New York: John Wiley & Sons, 1996.

Krugman, Paul. *The Great Unraveling: Losing Our Way in the New Century*. New York: W. W. Norton & Company, 2003.

Meltzer, Allan H. *A History of the Federal Reserve*. Chicago: University of Chicago Press, 2003.

Minsky, Hyman P. *John Maynard Keynes*. New York: McGraw-Hill, 2008.

————. *Stabilizing an Unstable Economy*. New York: McGraw-Hill, 2008.

Montier, James. *Behavioral Finance Insights into Irrational Minds and Markets*. New York: John Wiley & Sons, 2002.

Polanyi, Karl. *The Great Transformation: The Political and Economic Origins of Our Time.* Boston: Beacon Press, 1957.

Schumpeter, Joseph A. *Business Cycles: A Theoretical, Historical and Statistical Analysis of the Capitalist Process.* New York: McGraw-Hill, 1939.

_____. *Capitalism, Socialism and Democracy.* London: Allen & Unwin, 1976.

Shackle, G. L. S. *Expectations, Enterprise and Profit: The Theory of the Firm.* London: Allen & Unwin, 1970.

Shiller, Robert. *Irrational Exuberance.* Princeton: Princeton University Press, 2000).

Shleifer, Andrei. *Inefficient Markets: An Introduction to Behavioral Finance.* New York: Oxford University Press, 2000.

Solow, Robert M., and John B. Taylor. *Inflation, Unemployment, and Monetary Policy.* Cambridge: MIT Press, 1998.

Stiglitz, Joseph E. *The Roaring Nineties: A New History of the World's Most Prosperous Decade.* New York: W. W. Norton & Company, 2003.

Warsh, David. *Knowledge and the Wealth of Nations: A Story of Economic Discovery.* New York: W. W. Norton & Company, 2006.

Weintraub, E. Roy. *Microfoundations: The Compatibility of Microeconomics and Macroeconomics.* New York: Cambridge University Press, 1979.

Woodward, Bob. *Maestro: Greenspan's Fed and the American Boom.* New York: Simon and Schuster, 2000.

Articles

Akerlof, George A. "The Missing Motivation in Macroeconomics." Presidential Address, American Economic Association. Chicago, January 6, 2007.

Barbera, Robert J. "It's the Right Moment for the Minsky Model, The Elgar Companion to Minsky." Northhampton, Massachusetts: Edward Elgar Publishing, 2009.

————. "Boom, Gloom, and Excess." *International Economy*, Winter 2004.

————. "The Bursting of the Bubble in U.S. Technology Shares and the Deconstruction of Greenspan's Brave New World." Eleventh Annual Hyman P. Minsky Conference, April 2001.

————. "America's Bubble Budget." *Financial Times*, October 27, 2000.

————. "It Just Happened Again." Tenth Annual Hyman P. Minsky Conference, April 2000.

————. "Our Read on Bill Gates and Alan Greenspan at the White House." Commentary following participation in the White House Conference on the New Economy, *Strategic Investment Perspectives*, April 2000.

————. "The U.S. Trade Deficit as a Badge of Honor." Presented before the U.S. Senate Trade Deficit Review Commission, Washington, D.C., December 1999.

————. "Rates, Markets, and the Dollar: One View Shared with the CEA." Presented to the White House Council of Economic Advisors, November 1993.

————. "The End of Japan, Inc." Presented at the Jerome Levy Economics Institute of Bard College, Annual Public Policy Forum, November 1993.

————. "The Price of Money." *The Journal of Cash Management*, July 1993.

————. "An Economic Assessment: Contained Depression or the Foothills of a Recovery?" Public policy brief published by the Jerome Levy Economics Institute of Bard College, April 1992.

Bernanke, Ben S. "The Global Savings Glut and the Current Account Deficit." Speech delivered at the Sandridge lecture, Virginia Association of Economics, Richmond, Virginia, March 10, 2005.

Blanchard, Olivier. "What Do We Know About Macroeconomics That Fisher and Wicksell Did Not?" NBER Working Paper no. 7550, National Bureau of Economic Research, Massachusetts, February 2000.

Blinder, Alan S. "Is There a Core of Practical Macro That We Should All Believe?" *American Economic Review*, vol. 87, no. 2, May 1997.

Dynam, Karen E., and Donald L. Kohn. "The Rise in U.S. Household Indebtedness: Causes and Consequences." Paper prepared for the Federal Reserve Bank of Australia Conference, 2007, Federal Reserve Board, Washington, D.C., August 8, 2007.

Erturk, Korkut A. "On the Minskyan Business Cycle." Working Paper no. 474, Levy Institute of Bard College and University of Utah, New York, August 2006.

Goodfriend, Marvin. "Using Term Structure of Interest Rates for Monetary Policy." Federal Reserve Bank of Richmond, *Economic Quarterly*, Summer 1998, pp. 13-30.

Greenspan, Alan. "Risk and Uncertainty in Monetary Policy." Remarks at the meetings of the American Economic Association, San Diego, California, January 3, 2004.

Kregel, Jan A. "Understanding Imbalances in a Globalised International Economic System." Chapter from *Global Imbalances and the U.S. Debt Problem — Should Developing Countries Support the U.S. Dollar?* Fondad, The Hague, November 2006.

Liang, J. Nellie, and Steven A. Sharpe. "Share Repurchases and Employee Stock Options and Their Implications for S&P 500 Share Retirements and Expected Returns." Division of Research and Statistics, Federal Reserve Board, Washington, D.C., November 1999.

Mishkin, Frederick S. "Housing and the Monetary Transmission Mechanism." Prepared for the Federal Reserve Bank of Kansas City's 2007 Jackson Hole symposium, Jackson Hole, Wyoming, August 2007.

Pigeon, Marc-Andre. "It Happened, but Not Again: A Minskian Analysis of Japan's Lost Decade." Working Paper no. 303, Levy Institute of Bard College, New York, June 2000.

Romer, David. "Keynesian Macroeconomics Without the LM Curve." *Journal of Economic Perspectives*, vol. 14, no. 2, Spring 2000, pp.149-69.

Samuelson, Paul A. "Where Ricardo and Mill Rebut and Confirm Arguments of Mainstream Economist Supporting Globalization." *Journal of Economic Perspectives*, vol. 18, no. 3, Summer 2004, pp. 135-46.

Solow, Robert M. "Growth Theory and After." Lecture to the memory of Alfred Nobel, December 8, 1987.

Tymoigne, Eric. "The Minskyan System, Part I: Properties of the Minskyan Analysis and How to Theorize and Model a Monetary Production Economy." Working Paper no. 452, Levy Institute of Bard College, New York, June 2006.

―――. "The Minskyan System, Part II: Dynamics of the Minskyan Analysis and the Financial Fragility Hypothesis." Working Paper no. 453, Levy Institute of Bard College, New York, June 2006.

Weise, Charles. "A Simple Wicksellian Macroeconomic Model." *The B.E. Journal of Macroeconomics*, vol. 7, issue 1, article 11, May 29, 2007.

Weise, Charles, and Robert J. Barbera. "Minsky Meets Wicksell: Using the Wicksellian Model to Understand the Twenty-First Century Business Cycle" in Giuseppe Fontana and Mark Setterfield (eds.), *Macroeconomic Theory and Macroeconomic Pedagogy*. Basingstoke and New York: Palgrave Macmillan, forthcoming, Spring 2009.

Woodford, Michael. "Revolution and Evolution in Twentieth-Century Macroeconomics." Speech for the Conference on Frontiers of the Mind in the Twenty-First Century, Library of Congress, Washington, D.C., June 14-18, 1999.

INDEX

A

Accounts, maturity distribution of, 102

Adverse feedback loop, 101, 209

Africa, 59

AIG, 155

Asia
  asset markets, 93
  central banks, 130–131
  collapse (1997–1998), 19, 125
  currencies, 102
  economies, 94, 99, 104, 124
  financial mayhem, 6, 93–105
  markets, 103
  stocks, 101
  (*See also specific countries*)

Asset markets
  collapse in Japan, 98
  deflationary power of falling, 115
  excesses, 207
  ignored by Japan's policy makers, 96
  interplay with central banks and Main Street, 208
  as the main engines of cycles, 22
  policy of benign neglect toward, 79

Assets
  Asian, 95–96, 99–100, 181–182
  of banks, 34, 181–182
  houses as, 132
  prices, 20, 23, 41, 60, 117, 123
  risky, 48, 90–183

Attitudes toward risk, 32, 41, 142, 208–209

Austerity, global retrenchment and, 105

Automatic sell orders, 84–85

B

Bailouts, 22, 182

Balance sheets, cleaning up, 147

Bank(s)
  aggressively lending money, 132
  assets falling below liabilities, 34
  collapse during the Great Depression, 182
  equity of, 181
  failures, 181
  foreclosures as problems for, 33–36
  global bank run, 153, 156–157
  as not like other businesses, 182
  rescuing, 35–36
  run, avoided in Japan, 182

Bank of Japan, 98

Banking system
  creditworthiness of, 151
  crisis, free market ideologues and, 156
  industry deregulation, 87
  protecting, 36
  rescue plan, 157
  survival in Japan, 182

Bankruptcies, 35, 51, 58, 60, 144

Bear Stearns, 51–154

A Beautiful Mind, 198

Beggar my neighbor policies, 104–105

Behavioral economists, 185–186

Behavioral finance, 186

Benefits, in government projects, 57

Bernanke, Ben
  ahead of European Central Bank colleagues, 144
  angst about deficits (2006), 44–45
  on asset markets, 78
  Bernanke's calamity, 144–147
  casting a blind eye, 4

Bernanke, Ben (*Continued*)
efficient markets, 64
on financial crisis (2008), 146–147
on Greenspan's conundrum, 130
on ideologues in financial crises, 189
on interest rates, 21
mistakes of, 73
war against inflation, 19
Blind spots, 16
Bonds, safety of, 220
(*See also specific types of bonds*)
Boom and bust cycles
of the 1960s and 1970s, 16–18
boom without excesses, 77
and Chinese, 59
of free market economies, 163
in free market economy, 8
increasing risk leading to, 53–54
and investment, 7–8
of the last several decades, 15–23
Minsky on, 178
in Never Never Land, 38–39
primal causes of, 189
as tolerable, 167
in Wall Street and Washington, 2–3
Brave new world, 22, 107, 109, 117–119, 126–127
Bubbles
bubble budget, 201
burst, in Japan, 95, 98
housing bubble, 123–137, 185
investment bubbles, 108–110
recession as consequence of burst, 151
technology, 107–119
Budget surplus (2001), 198–202
Buffett, Warren, 214
Bush, George W., 182
Business cycle turning points, 40

Businesses (*See* Companies)
Buy or sell decisions, judging the future, 60

C

Capital, financing development in Asia, 59
Capital asset, price of, 60
Capital flows, engineering global boom, 63
Capital markets, 59–60, 62–63, 130
Capitalism, 3, 11
Capitalist economies, 7, 187
Capitalist finance, 2, 42, 55, 62–63
Capitalist instincts, of the Chinese, 60
Capitalist system, financial market mayhem, 152
Capital-to-labor ratio, 100
Carter, James Earl "Jimmy," 167
"Cash, at Long, Long Last, Is Trash," 90–91
Cash commitments, 40
Cash inflows, need for, 33–36
Central banks
arming with a new construct, 212–214
expanded role for, 11
fighting inflation (2007), 142–144
free hand at, 56
including asset prices in definition of stability, 23
interplay with asset markets and Main Street, 208
needing to pay attention to asset prices, 117
new consensus required, 207
problems from a global perspective, 206

raising interest rates (2004–05),
136
responding to increases in credit
spreads, 189
role of, 175
rules *versus* discretion at, 188
China
exports, 128, 135
foreign exchange reserves built
up by, 94
globalization, benefits of, 59
government spending on infrastructure, 214
investment explosion and growth
at risk, 93
keeping U.S. long rates low, 135
as master of vendor finance,
134–135
monetary policy, strategy for
conducting, 135
pegging currency to the U.S. dollar, 130
social infrastructure spending,
212
transformation after the death of
Mao, 60
Classical economists, 164–165, 170
Clean Water Act amendments of
1972, 193–194
Clinton, William Jefferson "Bill,"
20, 72
Collateralized mortgage obligations
(CDO), 132, 155–156
Commercial paper, 154, 157
Commodities, 144
Companies
borrowing costs, 136
confidence about business
prospects, 52–53
as too optimistic about revenue
inflows, 57

Competition, from new sources, 63
Complex mortgage products, 141
Confidence, 8, 43, 53, 146, 213
Congressional Budget Office
(CBO), 199
Consensus view, 46, 61, 65–68
Conservative economic thinking,
success of, 168
Conservative economists, 170
Consumer spending, 128, 134, 151
Continental sovereign bonds, 135
Conventional thinkers, forecasting
the past, 63–64
Conventional wisdom, 45–47, 116,
196–197
Conviction levels, 41, 47–48
Corporate bonds, 155
Corporations (*See* Companies)
Cost/benefit analysis, 57
Creative destruction, 10, 58, 63,
152, 171, 179–180, 182
Credit spreads (2004–05), 188–189
Crisis of 2008/2009 (*See under*
Financial crisis)
Currency, 100, 102
Cycles (*See* Financial cycles)

D

Debt
Asian borrowed in dollars,
99–100
deflation process, 147
excesses, 53
financing, 7
hedging, 41
magnifying gain and risk, 32
as private or sovereign, 102
servicing of, 40
(*See also* Mortgages)
Deflation, 20

Deflationary destruction, 152, 181
Demand, for houses, 150
Derivatives markets, 183
DeRosa, Paul, 216n1
Devaluation, prescribed by IMF in Asia, 104
Developed world, low interest rates to, 135–136
Disappointments, small, 32–33, 40, 54
Disintermediation, 87
Dollar/Chinese yuan exchange rate, 135
Dot-com IPO market, 22

E

Early years, of the author, 192–193
Earnings, raising the discounted value of, 219
Easy money, 124, 140
Easy-money-stoked boom, 125
Economic activity, and inflation rates, 168
Economic decline, reflecting flaws in capitalism, 165
Economic expansions, 4, 32
Economic forecasters, 46, 67
Economic growth, 17, 56
Economic health, 5
Economic hereafter, 45–46
Economic orthodoxy, 161–176
Economic performance, 61, 188
Economic policy, needing a new paradigm, 11
Economic predictions, 195
Economic prosperity, threats to, 205
Economic retrenchment, 41, 105, 115–116
Economic successes, in the 1980s, 5
Economic theoreticians, 9

Economic theory, mainstream, 73, 79, 88–89, 157, 207
Economic trends, 46
Economies, 162
Economists
    after Keynes, 166
    classical before Keynes, 164
    disregard for role of finance, 11
    excited about low wage and price inflation, 7
    groups of, 164–165
    as not generally trained in psychology, 185
    select group garnering attention, 195–196
    supporting the ECB, 144
E.F. Hutton, 195
Efficient market hypothesis, 60
Efficient markets, 63
Emerging nations, 135–136
Enthusiasm, lunatic levels, 43
Entrepreneurial risk taking, 179
Entrepreneurs, 10, 56, 187
Equilibriums, 63, 169
Equity, of banks, 34, 181
Equity markets, 98, 208
Equity share prices, 91
Europe, China's exports to, 135
European Central Bank (ECB), 79, 143
Excess
    in asset markets, 207
    defining, 20, 23, 73, 129
    economywide, 74
    in financial system, 56, 165, 206
    interest rates, 74–75
    risk taking, 152
    and success, 68
Exports, from China, 128, 135

F

Failure, keeping capital moving, 57
Faith, rekindling in finance,
    214–215
FDIC insurance, 182
Fed ease, witnessing dramatic, 90
Fed policy makers, 73–74, 129
Federal funds rate, 188
Federal Reserve Board
    AIG loan, 155
    Bear Stearns and JPMorgan
        Chase, 152–154
    collapsing overnight interest rates
        in 1987, 85
    Commercial Paper Funding
        Facility, 157
    deflation, 20
    focus on wages and prices, 20
    and inflation, 17, 19–20, 22,
        142–144, 167
    lowering interest rates, 116
    mistakes (mid-2000s), 131
    no recession forecast (July 2008),
        67
    raising interest rates (2000, 2004),
        114, 129
    raising rates at only a glacial
        pace, 129
    stepwise increases for Fed funds
        rate in 1980s, 88
Feedback mechanisms/loops, 64,
    101, 132–133, 139, 209
Finance
    as nonstop reassessment, 60–62
    rekindling faith in, 214–215
    simpler, transparent formulations,
        214–215
Finance practices, 20
Financial companies, as different,
    181

Financial crisis
    of 2008
        colossal scope of, 207
        coming to terms with, 10–11
        economic orthodoxy on the
            eve of, 161–176
        essential elements of, 149–151
        global policy risks in the
            aftermath of, 205–215
        response to, 1–2
        roots of, 207
        seeds of, 5
    of 2009, 104–105
    Bernanke on, 189
    in financial markets, 2, 5–6, 180
    government intervention,
        213–214
    Keynesian view, 179
Financial cycles, 21–23, 37
Financial innovation, 7
Financial instability, 7, 19, 37–54,
    83–92, 178, 186
Financial instability hypothesis, 32,
    40–43, 186
Financial institutions, 178
Financial leverage, 27, 29–31
Financial markets
    elevating to center stage, 208
    explosive trends ignored, 4
    ignored by monetary authorities,
        22
    as monetary policy mechanism,
        207–208
    punishing bubble-inflated sec-
        tors, 68
    as source of instability, 37–54, 78
    upheavals in, 6, 78
    violence in, 65
Financial relationships, tenuous
    nature of, 178
Financial speculation, 19

Financial survival constraint, 184
Financial system
  dynamics, 100
  excesses, 56, 165, 206
  introducing to Never Never
    Land, 39
Finnegan's Wake (Joyce), 202–203
Fiscal policy tools, 166
Fiscal stringency, in Asia, 104
Fixed rate mortgages (*See* Mort-
    gages)
Fleckenstein, William, 72–73
Forecasting, 46–47, 63–64, 196
Foreclosures, 33, 133, 141, 211
Foreign capital inflows, 206
Free market capitalism
  record over the past 50 years,
    186
  renewed commitment to, 2–4
  rewarding success, 108
  risk-taking entrepreneur as the
    driver, 187
  as superior, 55–69, 165
Free markets
  confidence in the infallibility of,
    4
  directing investment dollars, 59
  enthusiasts, 3–4
  faith in, 154
  fundamentalists, 165
  invisible hand of, 194
  outcomes, as infallible, 8
  processing information flawlessly,
    164
  systems, 57
Friedman, Milton, 166–168, 171,
    177
Frozen credit, 154–155
Frugality, mass move to, 209
Future, conjecture about, 43, 46,
    62

G

Gates, Bill, 72
Gazelle, meeting up with, 75–76
General Electric Company, 155
*The General Theory of Employment,
    Interest, and Money*
    (Keynes), 164
Germany, 212
Global bank run, 153, 156–157
Global capital markets mayhem,
    149
Global credit markets, 214
Global financial markets, 209
Global financial system, 206
Global Investment Prospects
    Conference, 97
Globalization, 59–60
Goldilocks economy/growth, 5, 7–8,
    15, 22, 41, 48–50, 79
Goldman Sachs, 156
Good times, 47–48, 50–52, 131,
    206
Government
  keeping small, 167
  moving forward on the back of
    big, 213–214
  redefining benefits, 57
  rescue by, 57
  role of, 152, 164
  stabilizing housing market,
    210
  visible hand of, 165, 182, 194,
    210–211
Government intervention, 170, 191,
    194
Great Depression, 143, 164, 170,
    181–183
Great Inflation, 22, 83, 170
Great Moderation, 5–6, 15–16, 21,
    76–78

Greenspan, Alan
  brave new world *vs.* irrational
    exuberance, 77
  budget surpluses as dangerously
    large, 43
  casting a blind eye, 4
  change of opinion about, 71–73
  confronting deep economic
    troubles, 117
  criticism of, 201
  efficient markets, 64
  envisioning complete payoff of
    federal debt, 218
  and financial crisis (2008), 71,
    183–184, 197
  Greenspan's conundrum,
    123–137, 144–147, 206
  idolatry of (2000), 72
  as ignorant, arrogant, naive and
    lazy, 72
  interest rate collapse (2001), 77
  irrational exuberance of U.S.
    equity markets, 76
  last war against inflation, 17–19
  markets assessing risk, 184–185
  mistake to lay blame solely on, 74
  mistakes of, 73
  not admitting flaws of financial
    architecture, 183
  policies (1990-91), 20
  puzzlement about interest rate
    dynamics, 21
  refusal to react to asset prices,
    123
  secular headwinds and debt
    excesses, 92
  suggesting robust economic
    growth (1990), 89
  White House speech, 111
Greenspan's Bubbles (Fleckenstein),
  72–73

Gross domestic product (GDP),
  168, 199–200
Growth/growth rates, 62, 74, 100,
  162–163

H

Happy yesterdays, 38, 47–48, 179,
  184
Hard fall, for housing, 140
Hedge finance stage, of capitalist
  finance, 42
Hedge fund, 218
Herds, 68, 109
High-yield paper, junk bonds as, 87
High-yield research, of Wall Street,
  88
Home buyers
  easier and easier ways to get
    credit, 131
  embracing risky financing strate-
    gies, 132
  evaluating a home purchase, 145
  fictional, buying first house, 26–36
  S&Ls lending money to, 87
  (*See also* Mortgages)
Home mortgage interest rates, 146,
  211
Home sales, slowing (2005), 141
House prices
  above fundamental values in
    many countries, 136
  driven higher by increase in de-
    mand, 133
  dynamic of falling, 141
  effects of rising and falling,
    209–210
  falling, 30, 140, 150
  linking to income, 26
  as never falling, 131–132
  rising, 27, 141

House prices (*Continued*)
   short-circuiting pessimism about,
      145
   surging, 132–134
   unprecedented climb in, 21
   up in every year since 1966,
      27–28
Households, 209–211
Houses, as asset, 132
Housing activity, 126–127, 140, 220
Housing bubble, 123–137,
      140–142, 185
Housing market, 41, 210–211, 220
Hussein, Saddam, 53, 89

I

IG Metall German union, 143
Income, linking home purchases to,
      26
Indonesia, 103–104
Infallible markets, belief in, 166
Inflation
   central banks fighting in 2007,
      142–144
   continuing to fight against, 16
   cycle *vs.* boom and bust, 7
   declining in the past 25 years, 15
   driving lower by crushing eco-
      nomic
      activity, 168
   Federal Reserve, 17, 19–20, 22,
      142–144, 167
   Great Inflation, 22, 83, 170
   Greenspan years, 17–19
   inflationary pressures, in expan-
      sions, 219
   lifting worldwide readings, 140
   low inflation rates, 124–125,
      168–169
   misguided focus on low, 115–117

rate of, compensation beyond, 219
   tamed (by 1998), 108
   vanquishment of, 17
Information, real world/financial
      market, 61
Innovation, 58, 63, 187
Instability, financial, 7, 19, 37–54,
      83–92, 178, 186
Insurance, on corporate bonds, 155
Interest rates
   bringing junk bond investments
      to default, 89
   as easy, 136
   falling raising share prices, 84
   keeping super low producing
      excesses, 74–75
   raised by Fed policy makers, 219
International borrowing, 102
International capital markets, 130
International Monetary Fund
      (IMF), 103–104
Investing, 26–29
Investment
   association with high rates of
      profit, 100
   booms, 19, 104
   bubbles, 108–110
   clustering of opportunities, 38
   Minsky move toward socializing,
      186
   in the real world, 37–38
Investment/financing-focused
      model, 7–8
Invisible hand, 162, 194
Irrational exuberance, 76–77, 185
Irrational Exuberance (Shiller), 109

J

Japan
   banks, 95

bubble popped by tight money, 98

collapse, 6, 19

falling values of bank assets, 181–182

as the global economic powerhouse, 97

home-grown growth required, 212

lost decade, 95, 99, 181–183

monetary policy leading to low long-term rates, 97

rise and collapse of, 94–95

Job losses (2008), 66

Jobless rate, during the Greenspan years, 17

John Maynard Keynes (Minsky), 177–179

Joyce, James, 202–203

JPMorgan Chase, 152

Junk bonds, 22, 86–87

K

Kaldor, Nicholas, 187

Keynes, John Maynard, 162, 164, 178, 208

Keynesian foundation, of Minsky, 176

Keynesian theory, 179

Keynesians, 164–166

Korean institutions, borrowing in dollars, 103

Krugman, Paul, 100–101

Kudlow, Larry, 218, 222

L

Labor market, 169, 174

Laffer, Arthur, 180–181

Lehman Brothers, 153–154, 156

Level playing field, for S&Ls, 87

Leverage, financial, 27, 29–31

Leveraged finance, 49

Leveraged wagers, 48–50

Liabilities, of banks, 34

Long-Term Capital Management (LTCM), 6, 124

Long-term expectations, 176

Long-term growth, tech stocks, 112–113

Long-term interest rates, 129–130

M

Macro forecasting models, 197

Macroeconomics

formulations, 194–196

foundations, 74

fundamentals of, 162–166

theories of, building in academia, 171

Madoff, Bernard L., 41

Maestro: Greenspan's Fed and the American Boom (Woodward), 72–73

Main Street, 7, 208

Mainstream economic theory, 73, 79, 88–89, 157, 207

Mainstream thinkers, 16, 79, 142

Malaysia, 103

Marathons, 75–76

Marginalization, of Minsky theories, 8–9

Margins of safety, 32, 40, 123, 187

Market judgments, wisdom of, 73

Market participants, changes not anticipated by, 64

Market strategy, triumph of, 55

Marketplace, making big bets in, 217

Markets, 55, 154, 166
  (*See also* Asset markets; Financial
      markets; Free markets)
Martin, William McChesney, 74
Mathematical models, 9
Mathematicians, models con-
    structed by, 9
Maturity distribution, of accounts,
    102
McCain, John, 72
Mehrling, Perry, 224
Mellon, Andrew, 143
Microeconomic foundations,
    193–194
Minsky, Hyman
  conclusions different from
      modern finance, 181, 185
  cost of capitalism, 63, 152,
      182–183
  economist wed to accounting
      concepts, 184
  expanding upon Schumpeter's
      ideas, 56
  finance as the key force for may-
      hem, 7–8
  financial instability hypothesis,
      186
  incorporating his vision, 79
  insights, 9–10, 32–33
  Keynes in a new light, 177–179
  margins of safety, 40
  meeting with, 91–92
  Minsky moments, 34–35, 88–90,
      149, 179
  model framework, 92, 183
  monetary policy and, 177–189
  pervasive uncertainty, 38, 45
  rising long rates alongside falling
      short rates, 147
  risk problem as systemic, 184
  stages of capitalist finance, 42

Taylor rule retrofit, 188
Mishkin, Frederick, 145
Mishkin strategy, 145–146
Modern finance, 184, 207
Monetarists, 164
Monetary authorities, tightening
    credit, 49
Monetary policy
  China strategy for conducting,
      135
  controlling the flow of money,
      167
  Great Moderation as a triumph
      for, 15–16
  ignoring market gains and credit
      finance, 10
  in Japan, 97
  in the late 1990s, 124
  making matters worse, 170–171
  Minsky and, 177–189
  New Keynesians design of,
      174–175
  Reagan revolution complement-
      ing, 169
  responsible for keeping inflation
      low, 168
  Shiller criticizing, 185
  Taylor rule, corresponding to, 188
  as transmission mechanism,
      207–208
Money market mutual funds, 154
Moral hazard, 88, 132
Mortgage originators, 132
Mortgage rates, 140–142, 145–146,
    211
Mortgages
  access to easy money, 124
  availability tightening, 150
  fixed rate not affected by Fed rate
      increases, 130
  fixed rate rising (2005–06), 140

fixed rate compared to 2–28
subprime, 31
fortunes made by Bear Stearns
on, 152
payments, not covered by
income, 28
slicing and dicing, 132

N

Nasdaq, 77, 116, 200
Nash, John Forbes, Jr., 198
National Association of Realtors,
27–28
Negative feedback, 103
Neoclassical synthesis, 164
Never Never Land, 38–40, 45, 48
New Keynesian economists,
174–175
News, immediate processing of, 62
Nikkei, 97–98
Nobel prizes, 166–167, 172, 177
Norris, Floyd, 201
Not-too-hot, not-too-cold (Goldilocks
economy/growth), 5, 7–8, 15,
22, 41, 48–50, 79

O

Oil prices, 144
O'Neill, Tip, 194–195
Opinion
bottom-up and top-down, 62
on Greenspan, 71–73
yesterday's news and current,
45–47, 179, 197

P

Parade of walking bankrupts, 35
Paradigm, new, 1–11, 165

Paradox of Goldilocks, 41, 48–50
P/E ratios, extreme, 109–110
Personal income taxes, cutting, 211
Pervasive uncertainty, 38, 45, 179,
195
Philippines, 103
Policy makers, blind spots, 16
Ponzi finance, 41–42, 149
Portfolio insurance, 84–86
Positive feedback loop, 132–133,
139
Post-Keynesian economists,
164–165, 175–176
Power, overestimated by the Fed,
73
Price levels, falling, 213
Price of labor, 169
Price/earnings ratios, 51–52
Prices, strategies depending on
climbing, 41
Profit growth, technology firms *vs.*
others, 111
Profits, as high indefinitely for Asian
economies, 100
Punch bowl, taking away, 74–76
Puzzles, focus on real world, 191

R

Rating agencies, 132
Rational expectations, 9, 167
Rational expectations school, 171,
223
Rational inhabitants, of Never
Never Land, 38–40
Raw industrial prices, 144
Reagan revolution, 8, 169
Real business cycle theory, 171–172
Real estate investment strategy, 32
Real rate, 219
Reassessment, finance as, 60–62

Recent past, 63–64, 68
Recessions
  capitulation after-the-fact (2008), 64–68
  as a consequence of a burst bubble, 151
  drivers of, 4
  entering (end of 2007), 151
  government role during, 169
  during the Greenspan years, 17–18
  labor markets and equilibrium during, 169
  mild nature (2001), 77
  predicting after arrival, 47
  rare and mild in the past 25 years, 15
Refinancing, 30, 34, 134
Regulation Q, 87
Rescue efforts, 57–58
Residential real estate collapse, 19
Retrenchment, 41, 56, 105, 115–116
Right brain thinking, 197–198
Rising markets, responding to, 189
Risk and risk taking
  appetites for, 37, 40, 206
  attitude toward, 32, 41, 142, 208–209
  as essential for economic growth, 94
  as free market driver, 4–5
  increasing coming naturally, 53–54
  and international borrowing, 102
  pricing of, 184
  in the stock market, 51–52
  and systemic risks, 186
Risky assets, 48, 90–183
Risky companies, 50–51, 136–137, 208

Risky finance
  basic concepts of, 25–36
  destabilizing consequences, 33
  embraced by home buyers, 132
  exaggerating small disappointments, 54
  flourishing as good times roll, 50–52
  getting riskier, 179
  happy yesterdays inviting, 47–48
  as the logical outcome of good times, 36
  mortgage products, 34
  recommiting to early in recoveries, 39
Robertson, Julian, 213, 217–218
Russia, 94, 124

S

Saddam Hussein, 53, 89
Safety margins, for nonbank financiers, 187
Samuelson, Paul, 47, 162, 178
Schumpeter, Joseph
  Ben Bernanke, 189
  coexist with Minsky visions (throughout the business cycle), 183
  creative destruction, 171
  dynamism of entrepreneurs, 56
  entrepreneurial risk taking, 179–180
  entrepreneurs in a capitalist system, 10
  unstable nature of capitalism, 63
Shiller, Robert, 109, 112, 185–186
Short-term borrowing, for longer-term projects, 102
Short-term interest rates, 129–130
S&L crisis, 6, 19, 86, 90

S&L industry, 86–88
Small disappointments, 32–33, 40, 54
Small setbacks, kicking off serious
    dislocations, 206
Social equity, 186
Socialized investment, 9–11, 57–59,
    187
Sociological insight, of Minsky, 32
Soft landing, 88–89, 115–117
South Korea, 103–104
Soviet Bloc, socialized investment
    as a failure, 58–59
Soviet Union, demise of, 8, 108
Speculation, increasing as expan-
    sions age, 41
Speculative finance stage, 42
Square root rule, 115
Stabilization strategies, 186
Stabilizing force, rational financiers
    as, 39
Status quo defenders (crisis of
    2008), 78–79
Stiglitz, Joseph E., 173
Stock market crash (1987), 6, 86
Stock market value, measures of, 109
Stock options, locking in, 84
Stock prices, 66, 84
Subprime borrowers, earning
    capital gains, 141
Subprime mortgages and loans, 22,
    29–30
Success, breeding excess, 68
Supply, of houses, rising, 150
Sustainable speeds, 75
Sweden, 157
Swiss National Bank, 157

T

Taiwan, 94
Tax rebates, 153, 211

Tax receipts, 199–200
Taylor, Washington, 173
Taylor rule, 175, 188
Teaser rate loans, 28, 140
Technology boom and bust cycle, 6,
    19, 54
Technology bubble, 107–119
Technology investment, 77
Technology share prices, 113
Technology start-ups, bankruptcies
    for, 20–21
Technology stocks, long-term
    growth, 112–113
Thailand, 102–104
Thrifts (*See* S&L crisis)
Tiger Fund, 218
Tight money, bursting technology
    bubble, 114
Time consistency literature, 223
Too big to fail doctrine, 182
Trade surplus, in Japan, 97
Treasury, U.K., 157
Treasury, U.S., 152–155, 157
Treasury bills, 135, 140, 154
Trends, extrapolating yesterday's,
    197
Truths, rediscovering, 208
Tsongas, Paul, 194

U

U.K. Treasury, 157
Unemployment, declining, 15
U.S. bonds, China purchasing,
    130
U.S. federal debt, complete payoff
    of, 218
U.S. Savings & Loan crisis
    (*See* S&L crisis)
U.S. Treasuries, 135, 140, 154
U.S. Treasury, 152–155, 157

V

Vendor finance, 134–135
Visible hand of government, 165,
    182, 210–211
Vogel, Ezra, 96
Volcker, Paul, 16–17, 167–168,
    194–195, 222

W

Wage rates, during recessions, 169
Wage-price spiral, 17
Wall Street
    cycle replacing inflationary boom
        and bust, 7
    designing its way into hyperrisky
        territory, 20
    finance, 23
    giving second tier status to, 208
    global banking business, 4
    innovation on, 187
    mortgages of questionable value,
        141

new financial instruments, 22
not holding junk bonds, 88
shining a spotlight on innovative
    approaches, 62
swings, 6
Wall Street Journal, 202–203
War, as a catalyst for recession, 53
Washington Mutual, 156
Wells, H.G., 202
White House Conference on the
    New Economy, 72, 109–110
Woodward, Bob, 72–73
World, as uncertain, 43–45, 88
Worldwide economy, limiting the
    damage to, 209

Y

Yesterday's news, informing current
    opinion, 45–47, 179, 197
Yuan-dollar exchange rate, 135

ABOUT THE AUTHOR

Dr. Robert J. Barbera is executive vice president and chief economist at ITG. He is responsible for ITG's global economic and financial market forecasts. Dr. Barbera has spent the last 26 years as a Wall Street economist, earning a wide institutional following. He is a frequent guest on CNBC and is regularly quoted in the *New York Times* and the *Wall Street Journal*.

Dr. Barbera currently is a Fellow in the Economics Department of the Johns Hopkins University. He has been teaching applied macroeconomics at Hopkins for the last five years.

Early in his career, Dr. Barbera served as a staff economist for U.S. senator Paul Tsongas and as an economist for the Congressional Budget Office. Dr. Barbera also lectured at MIT From mid-1994 through mid-1996, he was cochairman of Capital Investment International, a New York-based research boutique.

Dr. Barbera earned both his BA and Ph.D. from the Johns Hopkins University.